Abound Academy

Dedicated for your Abound success

Cisco Certified CyberOps Associate CBROPS 200-201 Mock Tests

Realistic Mock Tests with 380+ questions to get you CBROPS 200-201 certified

Abound Academy

Amazon Edition

About the Author

Abound Academy is a Professional Certification Provider Institution which provides content for major professional certification exams such as PMP®, Agile®, Disciplined Agile®, Scrum®, AWS®, Azure®, PSM®, and many other such high-demand certifications. We offer our candidates with exam study materials like online courses, training books, realistic mock questions, and downloadable pdf for all the resources that are featured in our Academy. We help you to boost your professional career by providing a definitive way of getting you certified on your respective certification on your very 1st attempt.

As an academy, we have enabled more than 100,000 individuals with their certification requirements and delivered successful results for more than 50,000 students. Our mission is to act as a stimulant to bring a positive boost in career change for everyone. Our study material and exam simulators are made to help the professionals to get certified, and thus achieve their goals in their respective fields.

We believe that skills and their certification has the power to transform lives and the whole world. We are dedicated to providing best-in-industry training and mock tests that are delivered by highly experienced and competent industry experts. We thrive to work in partnership with communities over the boundaries. Our focus is to become the leading provider of high-quality online certification training to professionals over the boundaries.

Table of Content

Chapter 1: Introduction

As the sophistication, stealth, and frequency of cybersecurity threats continue to increase, the complexity of attacks means every organization needs security expertise before, during, and after an attack. For this reason, the demand for cybersecurity operations (CyberOps) personnel keeps going up.

The updated Cisco Certified CyberOps Associate certification program validates the day-to-day, tactical knowledge and skills that Security Operations Center (SOC) teams need to detect and respond to cybersecurity threats. The certification validates the fundamentals needed for associate-level job roles, with one exam and one training course to help you prepare. The exam and training cover knowledge and skills related to security concepts, security monitoring, host based analysis, network intrusion analysis, and security policies and procedures.

From a recognized provider of security solutions and certifications, the CyberOps Associate certification and training program is your pathway to a career in cybersecurity operations. And the process couldn't be simpler: pass one exam and you are on your way.

1.1 Benefits

- **Launch your career in cybersecurity operations** with the Cisco® Certified CyberOps Associate certification
- **Master the essentials** to prevent, detect, and respond to cybersecurity threats and breaches

- **Rev up your resume** with training and certification on cybersecurity operations knowledge and skills
- **Boost your confidence** by gaining real-world knowledge
- **Tell the world what you have achieved** with a digital certification badge on your social media profiles

The updated Cisco CyberOps Associate training and certification program prepares you for an associate-level job role so you can prevent, detect, and defend against cybersecurity threats. The program can launch your career, by showing hiring managers you have the real-world knowledge and skills to be a valuable member of any SOC team.

To earn the CyberOps Associate certification, you pass one exam. The 200-201 Understanding Cisco Cybersecurity Operations Fundamentals (CBROPS) exam, focuses on your knowledge of associate level cyber operations including security concepts, security monitoring, host-based analysis, network intrusion analysis, and security policies and procedures.

The Understanding Cisco Cybersecurity Operations Fundamentals (CBROPS) course prepares you to pass the exam with practical skills you can apply to jobs in cybersecurity.

Cisco Certified CyberOps Associate certification can launch your career. Certify your CyberOps skills and show hiring managers that you have the real-world know-how to prevent, detect, and defend their networks against cybersecurity threats.

1.2 Exam Details

Exam Name	Cisco Certified CyberOps Associate
Exam Number	200-201 CBROPS
Exam Description	The CBROPS exam tests a candidate's knowledge and skills related to security concepts, security monitoring, host-based analysis, network intrusion analysis, and security policies and procedures.
Exam Price	$300 USD
Duration	120 minutes
Number of Questions	95 - 105
Passing Score	Variable (750-850 / 1000 Approx.)

1.3 Domains Covered

Topics	Percentage covered
Security Concepts	20%
Security Monitoring	25%
Host-Based Analysis	20%
Network Intrusion Analysis	20%
Security Policies and Procedures	15%
Total	**100%**

Chapter 2: 200-201 CBROPS Mock Test #1

Question 1:
What is the purpose of entering the nslookup cisco.com command on a Windows PC?
  A. to check if the DNS service is running
  B. to connect to the Cisco server
  C. to test if the Cisco server is reachable
  D. to discover the transmission time needed to reach the Cisco server

Answer: A.

Explanation
The nslookup command queries DNS servers to find out the IP address or addresses associated with the domain name cisco.com. A successful result indicates that the DNS configuration on the PC is functional, and also indicates the IP address for the domain name being displayed. The command does not try to connect to the actual Cisco host directly.

Question 2:
How is the event ID assigned in Sguil?
  A. All events ¡n the series of correlated events are assigned the same event ID.
  B. Only the first event in the series of correlated events is assigned a unique ID.
  C. All events in the series of correlated events are assigned the same event group ID.
  D. Each event in the series of correlated events is assigned a unique

Answer: D.

Explanation
In Sguil, each event receives a unique event ID, but only the first event ID in the series of correlated events is displayed in the RealTime tab

Question 3:
Which two types of network traffic are from protocols that generate a lot of routine traffic? (Choose two.)
  A. routing updates traffic
  B. Windows security auditing alert traffic
  C. IPsec traffic
  D. STP traffic
  E. SSLtraffic

Answer: A, D.

Explanation

To reduce the huge amount of data collected so that cybersecurity analysts can focus on critical threats, some less important or less relevant data could be eliminated from the datasets. For example, routing network management traffic, such as routing updates and STP traffic, could be eliminated.

Question 4:
What are two elements that form the PRI value in a syslog message? (Choose two.)
   A. facility
   B. timestamp
   C. severity
   D. header
   E. host name

Answer: A, C.

Explanation
The PRI in a syslog message consists of two elements, the facility and severity of the message.

Question 5:
Which three pieces of information are found in session data? (Choose three.)
   A. default gateway IP address
   B. source and destination port numbers
   C. Layer 4 transport protocol
   D. source and destination MAC addresses
   E. user name
   F. source and destination IP addresses

Answer: B, C, F.

Explanation
Session data includes identifying information such as source and destination IP addresses, source and destination port numbers, and the Layer 4 protocol in use. Session data does not include user name, source and destination MAC addresses, and a default gateway IP address.

Question 6:
What kind of ICMP message can be used by threat actors to perform network reconnaissance and scanning attacks?
   A. ICMP mask reply
   B. ICMP router discovery
   C. ICMP unreachable
   D. ICMP redirects

Answer: C.

Explanation

Common ICMP messages of interest to threat actors includes :
- the ICMP echo request and echo reply,
- used to perform host verification and DoS attacks ICMP unreachable
- used to perform network reconnaissance and scanning attacks ICMP mask reply
- used to map an internal IP network ICMP redirects
- used to lure a target host Into sending all traffic through a compromised device and create a man-in-the-middle attack ICMP router discovery
- used to inject bogus route entries into the routing table of a target host

Question 7:
A flood of packets with invalid source IP addresses requests a connection on the network. The server busily tries to respond, resulting in valid requests being ignored. What type of attack has occurred?
    A. TCP session hijacking
    B. TCP SYN flood
    C. TCP reset
    D. UDP flood

Answer: B.

Explanation

The TCP SYN Flood attack exploits the TCP three-way handshake. The threat actor continually sends TCP SYN session request packets with a randomly spoofed source IP address to an intended target. The target device replies with a TCP SYN-ACK packet to the spoofed IP address and waits for a TCP ACK packet. Those responses never arrive. Eventually the target host is overwhelmed with half-open TCP connections and denies TCP services.

Question 8:
An attacker is redirecting traffic to a false default gateway in an attempt to intercept the data traffic of a switched network. What type of attack could achieve this?
    A. DNS tunneling
    B. TCP SYN flood
    C. DHCP spoofing
    D. ARP cache poisoning

Answer: C.

Explanation

In DHCP spoofing attacks, a threat actor configures a fake DHCP server on the network to issue DHCP addresses to clients with the aim of forcing the clients to use a false or invalid default gateway. A man-in-the-middle attack can be created by setting the default gateway address to the IP address of the threat actor.

Question 9:
What is the most common goal of search engine optimization (SEO) poisoning?
- A. to increase web traffic to malicious sites
- B. to build a botnet of zombies
- C. to trick someone into installing malware or divulging personal information
- D. to overwhelm a network device with maliciously formed packets

Answer: A.

Explanation

A malicious user could create a SEO so that a malicious website appears higher in search results. The malicious website commonly contains malware or is used to obtain information via social engineering techniques.

Question 10:
Users report that a database file on the main server cannot be accessed. A database administrator verifies the issue and notices that the database file is now encrypted. The organization receives a threatening email demanding payment for the decryption of the database file. What type of attack has the organization experienced?
- A. man-in-the-middle attack
- B. DoS attack
- C. ransomware
- D. Trojan horse

Answer: C.

Explanation

A cybersecurity specialist needs to be familiar with the characteristics of the different types of malware and attacks that threaten an organization.

Question 11:
What two kinds of personal information can be sold on the dark web by cybercriminals? (Choose two.)
- A. city of residence
- B. Facebook photos
- C. name of a bank
- D. name of a pet
- E. street address

Answer: B, E.

Explanation

Personally identifiable information (PII) is any information that can be used to positively identify an individual. Examples of PII include the following: Name Social security number Birth Date

Credit card numbers Bank account numbers Facebook information Address information (street, email, phone numbers).

Question 12:
What three services are offered by FireEye? (Choose three.)
    A. blocks attacks across the web
    B. creates firewall rules dynamically
    C. identifies and stops latent malware on files
    D. subjects all traffic to deep packet inspection analysis
    E. deploys incident detection rule sets to network security tools
    F. identifies and stops email threat vectors

Answer: A, C, F.

Explanation
FireEye is a security company that uses a three-pronged approach combining security intelligence, security expertise, and technology. FireEye offers SIEM and SOAR with the Helix Security Platform, which uses behavioral analysis and advanced threat detection.

Question 13:
After containment, what is the first step of eradicating an attack?
    A. Change all passwords.
    B. Patch all vulnerabilities.
    C. Hold meetings on lessons learned.
    D. Identify all hosts that need remediation.

Answer: D.

Explanation
Once an attack is contained, the next step is to identify all hosts that will need remediation so that the effects of the attack can be eliminated.

Question 14:
Which activity is typically performed by a threat actor in the installation phase of the Cyber Kill Chain?
    A. Install a web shell on the target web server for persistent access.
    B. Harvest email addresses of user accounts.
    C. Open a two-way communication channel to the CnC infrastructure.
    D. Obtain an automated tool to deliver the malware payload.

Answer: A.

Explanation

In the installation phase of the Cyber Kill Chain, the threat actor establishes a backdoor into the system to allow for continued access to the target.

Question 15:

When dealing with a security threat and using the Cyber Kill Chain model, which two approaches can an organization use to help block potential exploitations on a system? (Choose two.)

    A. Collect email and web logs for forensic reconstruction.
    B. Conduct full malware analysis.
    C. Train web developers for securing code.
    D. Build detections for the behavior of known weaponizers.
    E. Perform regular vulnerability scanning and penetration testing.

Answer: C, E.

Explanation
The most common exploit targets, once a weapon is delivered, are applications, operating system vulnerabilities, and user accounts. Among other measures, such as regular vulnerability scanning and penetration testing, training web developers in securing code can help block potential exploitations on systems.

Question 16:

How might corporate IT professionals deal with DNS-based cyber threats?

    A. Limit the number of simultaneously opened browsers or browser tabs.
    B. Monitor DNS proxy server logs and look for unusual DNS queries.
    C. Use IPS/IDS devices to scan internal corporate traffic.
    D. Limit the number of DNS queries permitted within the organization.

Answer: B.

Explanation
DNS queries for randomly generated domain names or extremely long random-appearing DNS subdomains should be considered suspicious. Cyberanalysts could do the following for DNS-based attacks: Analyze DNS logs. Use a passive DNS service to block requests to suspected CnC and exploit domains.

Question 17:

How does using HTTPS complicate network security monitoring?

    A. HTTPS adds complexity to captured packets.
    B. HTTPS cannot protect visitors to a company-provided web site.
    C. Web browser traffic is directed to infected servers.
    D. HTTPS can be used to infiltrate DNS queries.

Answer: A.

Explanation

HTTPS adds extra overhead to the HTTP-formed packet. HTTPS encrypts using a secure socket layer (SSL). Even though some devices can perform SSL decryption and inspection, this can present processing and privacy issues. HTTPS adds complexity to packet captures due to the additional message involved in establishing an encrypted data connection.

Question 18:

What are the two important components of a public key infrastructure (PKI) used in network security? (Choose two.)
  A. intrusion prevention system
  B. digital certificates
  C. symmetric encryption algorithms
  D. certificate authority
  E. pre-shared key generation

Answer: B, D.

Explanation

A public key infrastructure uses digital certificates and certificate authorities to manage asymmetric key distribution. PKI certificates are public information. The PKI certificate authority (CA) is a trusted third-party that issues the certificate. The CA has its own certificate (self-signed certificate) that contains the public key of the CA.

Question 19:

Which three algorithms are designed to generate and verify digital signatures? (Choose three.)
  A. 3DES
  B. IKE
  C. DSA
  D. AES
  E. ECDSA
  F. RSA

Answer: C, E, F.

Explanation

There are three Digital Signature Standard (DSS) algorithms that are used for generating and verifying digital signatures: Digital Signature Algorithm (DSA) Rivest-Shamir Adleman Algorithm (RSA) Elliptic Curve Digital Signature Algorithm (ECDSA)

Question 20:

Which section of a security policy is used to specify that only authorized individuals should have access to enterprise data?

A. statement of authority
B. identification and authentication policy
C. campus access policy
D. Internet access policy
E. statement of scope
F. acceptable use policy

Answer: B.

Explanation
The identification and authentication policy section of the security policy typically specifies authorized persons that can have access to network resources and identity verification procedures.

Question 21:
What kind of message is sent by a DHCPv4 client requesting an IP address?
   A. DHCPDISCOVER broadcast message
   B. DHCPDISCOVER unicast message
   C. DHCPOFFER unicast message
   D. DHCPACK unicast message

Answer: A.

Explanation
When the DHCPv4 client requests an IP address, it sends a DHCPDISCOVER broadcast message seeking a DHCPv4 server on the network.

Question 22:
What is the responsibility of the human resources department when handling a security incident?
   A. Coordinate the incident response with other stakeholders and minimize the damage of the incident.
   B. Perform actions to minimize the effectiveness of the attack and preserve evidence.
   C. Apply disciplinary measures if an incident is caused by an employee.
   D. Review the incident policies, plans, and procedures for local or federal guideline violations.

Answer: C.

Explanation
The human resources department may be called upon to perform disciplinary measures if an incident is caused by an employee.

Question 23:

How does a security information and event management system (SIEM) in a SOC help the personnel fight against security threats?
   A. by integrating all security devices and appliances in an organization
   B. by analyzing logging data in real time
   C. by combining data from multiple technologies
   D. by dynamically implementing firewall rules

Answer: C.

Explanation
A security information and event management system (SIEM) combines data from multiple sources to help SOC personnel collect and filter data, detect and classify threats, analyze and investigate threats, and manage resources to implement preventive measures.

Question 24:
At which OSI layer is a source IP address added to a PDU during the encapsulation process?
   A. network layer
   B. transport layer
   C. data link layer
   D. application layer

Answer: A.

Explanation
CSMA/CA stands for carrier sense multiple access with collision avoidance. It is a mechanism used in wireless networks to prevent packet collisions from occurring.

Question 25:
What is the purpose of CSMA/CA?
   A. to prevent loops
   B. to isolate traffic
   C. to filter traffic
   D. to prevent collisions

Answer: D.

Explanation
CSMA/CA stands for carrier sense multiple access with collision avoidance. It is a mechanism used in wireless networks to prevent packet collisions from occurring.

Question 26:
Why is DHCP preferred for use on large networks?

A. Hosts on large networks require more IP addressing configuration settings than hosts on small networks.
B. It prevents sharing of files that are copyrighted.
C. It is a more efficient way to manage IP addresses than static address assignment.
D. Large networks send more requests for domain to IP address resolution than do smaller networks.
E. DHCP uses a reliable transport layer protocol.

Answer: C, E.

Explanation
Static IP address assignment requires personnel to configure each network host with addresses manually. Large networks can change frequently and have many more hosts to configure than do small networks. DHCP provides a much more efficient means of configuring and managing IP addresses on large networks than does static address assignment.

Question 27:
Which NIST incident response life cycle phase includes continuous monitoring by the CSIRT to quickly identify and validate an incident?
A. postincident activities
B. detection and analysis
C. containment, eradication, and recovery
D. preparation

Answer: B.

Explanation
It is in the detection and analysis phase of the NIST incident response life cycle that the CSIRT identifies and validates incidents through continuous monitoring. The NIST defines four stages of the incident response life cycle.

Question 28:
What will a threat actor do to create a back door on a compromised target according to the Cyber Kill Chain model?
A. Add services and autorun keys.
B. Collect and exfiltrate data.
C. Obtain an automated tool to deliver the malware payload.
D. Open a two-way communications channel to the CnC infrastructure.

Answer: A.

Explanation

Once a target system is compromised, the threat actor will establish a backdoor into the system to allow for continued access to the target. Adding services and autorun keys is a way to create a point of persistent access.

Question 29:
Which type of evidence supports an assertion based on previously obtained evidence?
    A. direct evidence
    B. corroborating evidence
    C. best evidence
    D. indirect evidence

Answer: B.

Explanation
Corroborating evidence is evidence that supports a proposition already supported by initial evidence, therefore confirming the original proposition. Circumstantial evidence is evidence other than first-hand accounts of events provided by witnesses.

Question 30:
A technician is configuring email on a mobile device. The user wants to be able to keep the original email on the server, organize it into folders, and synchronize the folders between the mobile device and the server. Which email protocol should the technician use?
    A. POP3
    B. MIME
    C. IMAP
    D. SMTP

Answer: C.

Explanation
The IMAP protocol allows email data to be synchronized between a client and server. Changes made in one location, such as marking an email as read, are automatically applied to the other location. POP3 is also an email protocol. However, the data is not synchronized between the client and the server. SMTP is used for sending email, and is typically used in conjunction with the POP3 protocol. MIME is an email standard that is used to define attachment types, and allows extra content like pictures and documents to be attached to email messages.

Question 31:
What is the goal of an attack in the installation phase of the Cyber Kill Chain?
    A. Break the vulnerability and gain control of the target.
    B. Establish command and control (CnC) with the target system.
    C. Create a backdoor in the target system to allow for future access.

D. Use the information from the reconnaissance phase to develop a weapon against the target.

Answer: C.

Explanation
In the installation phase of the Cyber Kill Chain, the threat actor establishes a backdoor into the system to allow for continued access to the target.

Question 32:
Which two statements are characteristics of a virus? (Choose two.)
  A. A virus typically requires end-user activation.
  B. A virus can be dormant and then activate at a specific time or date.
  C. A virus replicates itself by independently exploiting vulnerabilities in networks.
  D. A virus has an enabling vulnerability, a propagation mechanism, and a payload.
  E. A virus provides the attacker with sensitive data, such as passwords.

Answer: A, B.

Explanation
The type of end user interaction required to launch a virus is typically opening an application, opening a web page, or powering on the computer. Once activated, a virus may infect other files located on the computer or other computers on the same network.

Question 33:
What is a characteristic of a Trojan horse as it relates to network security?
  A. Too much information is destined for a particular memory block, causing additional memory areas to be affected.
  B. Extreme quantities of data are sent to a particular network device interface.
  C. An electronic dictionary is used to obtain a password to be used to infiltrate a key network device.
  D. Malware is contained in a seemingly legitimate executable program.

Answer: D.

Explanation
A Trojan horse carries out malicious operations under the guise of a legitimate program. Denial of service attacks send extreme quantities of data to a particular host or network device interface. Password attacks use electronic dictionaries in an attempt to learn passwords. Buffer overflow attacks exploit memory buffers by sending too much information to a host to render the system inoperable.

Question 34:
What technique is used in social engineering attacks?

A. sending junk email
B. buffer overflow
C. phishing
D. man-in-the-middle

Answer: C.

Explanation
A threat actor sends fraudulent email which is disguised as being from a legitimate, trusted source to trick the recipient into installing malware on their device, or to share personal or financial information.

Question 35:
What is the purpose of implementing VLANs on a network?
A. They can separate user traffic.
B. They prevent Layer 2 loops.
C. They eliminate network collisions.
D. They allow switches to forward Layer 3 packets without a router.

Answer: A.

Explanation
VLANs are used on a network to separate user traffic based on factors such as function, project team, or application, without regard for the physical location of the user or device.

Question 36:
A cybersecurity analyst needs to collect alert data. What are three detection tools to perform this task in the Security Onion architecture? (Choose three.)
A. CapME
B. Wazuh
C. Kibana
D. Zeek
E. Sguil
F. Wireshark

Answer: A, B, D.

Question 37:
In addressing an identified risk, which strategy aims to shift some of the risk to other parties?
A. risk avoidance
B. risk sharing
C. risk retention
D. risk reduction

Answer: B.

Question 38:
What is a network tap?
    A. a technology used to provide real-time reporting and long-term analysis of security events
    B. a Cisco technology that provides statistics on packets flowing through a router or multilayer switch
    C. a feature supported on Cisco switches that enables the switch to copy frames and forward them to an analysis device
    D. a passive device that forwards all traffic and physical layer errors to an analysis device

Answer: D.

Explanation
A network tap is used to capture traffic for monitoring the network. The tap is typically a passive splitting device implemented inline on the network and forwards all traffic, including physical layer errors, to an analysis device.

Question 39:
If a SOC has a goal of 99.999% uptime, how many minutes of downtime a year would be considered within its goal?
    A. Approximately 5 minutes per year.
    B. Approximately 10 minutes per year
    C. Approximately 20 minutes per year.
    D. Approximately 30 minutes per year.

Answer: A.

Explanation
Within a year, there are 365 days x 24 hours a day x 60 minutes per hour = 525,600 minutes. With the goal of uptime 99.999% of time, the downtime needs to be controlled under 525,600 x (1-0.99999) = 5.256 minutes a year.

Question 40:
The HTTP server has responded to a client request with a 200 status code. What does this status code indicate?
    A. The request is understood by the server, but the resource will not be fulfilled.
    B. The request was completed successfully.
    C. The server could not find the requested resource, possibly because of an incorrect URL.
    D. The request has been accepted for processing, but processing is not completed.

Answer: B.

Question 41:
What is an advantage for small organizations of adopting IMAP instead of POP?
  A. POP only allows the client to store messages in a centralized way, while IMAP allows distributed storage.
  B. IMAP sends and retrieves email, but POP only retrieves email.
  C. When the user connects to a POP server, copies of the messages are kept in the mail server for a short time, but IMAP keeps them for a long time.
  D. Messages are kept in the mail servers until they are manually deleted from the email client.

Answer: D.

Explanation
IMAP and POP are protocols that are used to retrieve email messages. The advantage of using IMAP instead of POP is that when the user connects to an IMAP-capable server, copies of the messages are downloaded to the client application. IMAP then stores the email messages on the server until the user manually deletes those messages.

Question 42:
What debugging security tool can be used by black hats to reverse engineer binary files when writing exploits?
  A. WinDbg
  B. Firesheep
  C. Skipfish
  D. AIDE

Answer: A.

Question 43:
What are two features of ARP? (Choose two.)
  A. When a host is encapsulating a packet into a frame, it refers to the MAC address table to determine the mapping of IP addresses to MAC addresses.
  B. If a host is ready to send a packet to a local destination device and it has the IP address but not the MAC address of the destination, it generates an ARP broadcast.
  C. If a device receiving an ARP request has the destination IPv4 address, it responds with an ARP reply.
  D. If no device responds to the ARP request, then the originating node will broadcast the data packet to all devices on the network segment.
  E. An ARP request is sent to all devices on the Ethernet LAN and contains the IP address of the destination host and the multicast MAC address.

Answer: B, C.

Explanation

When a node encapsulates a data packet into a frame, it needs the destination MAC address. First it determines if the destination device is on the local network or on a remote network. Then it checks the ARP table (not the MAC table) to see if a pair of IP address and MAC address exists for either the destination IP address (if the destination host is on the local network) or the default gateway IP address (if the destination host is on a remote network).

If the match does not exist, it generates an ARP broadcast to seek the IP address to MAC address resolution. Because the destination MAC address is unknown, the ARP request is broadcast with the MAC address FFFF.FFFF.FFFF. Either the destination device or the default gateway will respond with its MAC address, which enables the sending node to assemble the frame. If no device responds to the ARP request, then the originating node will discard the packet because a frame cannot be created.

Question 44:
What is a property of the ARP table on a device?
    A. Entries in an ARP table are time-stamped and are purged after the timeout expires.
    B. Every operating system uses the same timer to remove old entries from the ARP cache.
    C. Static IP-to-MAC address entries are removed dynamically from the ARP table.
    D. Windows operating systems store ARP cache entries for 3 minutes.

Answer: A.

Question 45:
What is the purpose of Tor?
    A. to allow users to browse the Internet anonymously
    B. to securely connect to a remote network over an unsecure link such as an Internet connection
    C. to donate processor cycles to distributed computational tasks in a processor sharing P2P network
    D. to inspect incoming traffic and look for any that violates a rule or matches the signature of a known exploit

Answer: A.

Explanation

Tor is a software platform and network of peer-to-peer (P2P) hosts that function as routers. Users access the Tor network by using a special browser that allows them to browse anonymously.

Question 46:
Which two network protocols can be used by a threat actor to exfiltrate data in traffic that is disguised as normal network traffic? (Choose two.)
    A. NTP
    B. DNS

C. HTTP
D. syslog
E. SMTP

Answer: B, C.

Question 47:
What is a key difference between the data captured by NetFlow and data captured by Wireshark?
    A. NetFlow data shows network flow contents whereas Wireshark data shows network flow statistics.
    B. NetFlow data is analyzed by tcpdump whereas Wireshark data is analyzed by nfdump.
    C. NetFlow provides transaction data whereas Wireshark provides session data.
    D. NetFlow collects metadata from a network flow whereas Wireshark captures full data packets.

Answer: D.

Explanation
Wireshark captures the entire contents of a packet. NetFlow does not. Instead, NetFlow collects metadata, or data about the flow.

Question 48:
Which tool captures full data packets with a command-line interface only?
    A. nfdump
    B. Wireshark
    C. NBAR2
    D. tcpdump

Answer: D.

Explanation
The command-line tool tcpdump is a packet analyzer. Wireshark is a packet analyzer with a GUI interface.

Question 49:
Which method can be used to harden a device?
    A. maintain use of the same passwords
    B. allow default services to remain enabled
    C. allow USB auto-detection
    D. use SSH and disable the root account access over SSH

Answer: D.

Explanation

The basic best practices for device hardening are as follows:
- Ensure physical security.
- Minimize installed packages.
- Disable unused services.
- Use SSH and disable the root account login over SSH.
- Keep the system updated.
- Disable USB auto-detection.
- Enforce strong passwords.
- Force periodic password changes.
- Keep users from reusing old passwords.
- Review logs regularly.

Question 50:

In a Linux operating system, which component interprets user commands and attempts to execute them?
- A. GUI
- B. daemon
- C. kernel
- D. shell

Answer: D.

Question 51:

A network administrator is configuring an AAA server to manage RADIUS authentication. Which two features are included in RADIUS authentication? (Choose two.)
- A. encryption for all communication
- B. encryption for only the data
- C. single process for authentication and authorization
- D. separate processes for authentication and authorization
- E. hidden passwords during transmission

Answer: C, E.

Explanation

RADIUS authentication supports the following features: RADIUS authentication and authorization as one process Encrypts only the password Utilizes UDP Supports remote-access technologies, 802.1X, and Session Initiation Protocol (SIP)

Question 52:

What is privilege escalation?
- A. Vulnerabilities in systems are exploited to grant higher levels of privilege than someone or some process should have.

B. Everyone is given full rights by default to everything and rights are taken away only when someone abuses privileges.
C. Someone is given rights because she or he has received a promotion.
D. A security problem occurs when high ranking corporate officials demand rights to systems or files that they should not have.

Answer: A.

Explanation
With privilege escalation, vulnerabilities are exploited to grant higher levels of privilege. After the privilege is granted, the threat actor can access sensitive information or take control of the system.

Question 53:
What two assurances does digital signing provide about code that is downloaded from the Internet? (Choose two.)
   A. The code contains no viruses.
   B. The code has not been modified since it left the software publisher.
   C. The code is authentic and is actually sourced by the publisher.
   D. The code contains no errors.
   E. The code was encrypted with both a private and public key.

Answer: B, C.

Explanation
Digitally signing code provides several assurances about the code: The code is authentic and is actually sourced by the publisher. The code has not been modified since it left the software publisher. The publisher undeniably published the code. This provides nonrepudiation of the act of publishing.

Question 54:
Which approach can help block potential malware delivery methods, as described in the Cyber Kill Chain model, on an Internet-faced web server?
   A. Build detections for the behavior of known malware.
   B. Collect malware files and metadata for future analysis.
   C. Audit the web server to forensically determine the origin of the exploit.
   D. Analyze the infrastructure storage path used for files.

Answer: D.

Explanation
A threat actor may send the weapon through web interfaces to the target server, either in file uploads or coded web requests. By analyzing the infrastructure storage path used for files,

security measures can be implemented to monitor and detect malware deliveries through these methods.

Question 55:

Which measure can a security analyst take to perform effective security monitoring against network traffic encrypted by SSL technology?
- A. Use a Syslog server to capture network traffic.
- B. Deploy a Cisco SSL Appliance.
- C. Require remote access connections through IPsec VPN.
- D. Deploy a Cisco ASA.

Answer: C.

Question 56:

An administrator is trying to develop a BYOD security policy for employees that are bringing a wide range of devices to connect to the company network. Which three objectives must the BYOD security policy address? (Choose three.)
- A. All devices must be insured against liability if used to compromise the corporate network.
- B. All devices must have open authentication with the corporate network.
- C. Rights and activities permitted on the corporate network must be defined.
- D. Safeguards must be put in place for any personal device being compromised.
- E. The level of access of employees when connecting to the corporate network must be defined.
- F. All devices should be allowed to attach to the corporate network flawlessly.

Answer: C, D, E.

Question 57:

What type of attack targets an SQL database using the input field of a user?
- A. XML injection
- B. buffer overflow
- C. Cross-site scripting
- D. SQL injection

Answer: D.

Explanation
A criminal can insert a malicious SQL statement in an entry field on a website where the system does not filter the user input correctly.

Question 58:

What are two characteristics of Ethernet MAC addresses? (Choose two.)
- A. MAC addresses use a flexible hierarchical structure.
- B. They are expressed as 12 hexadecimal digits.

C. They are globally unique.
D. They are routable on the Internet.
E. MAC addresses must be unique for both Ethernet and serial interfaces on a device.

Answer: B, C.

Question 59:

A user calls to report that a PC cannot access the internet. The network technician asks the user to issue the command ping 127.0.0.1 in a command prompt window. The user reports that the result is four positive replies. What conclusion can be drawn based on this connectivity test?
   A. The IP address obtained from the DHCP server is correct.
   B. The PC can access the network. The problem exists beyond the local network.
   C. The PC can access the Internet. However, the web browser may not work.
   D. The TCP/IP implementation is functional.

Answer: D.

Question 60:

What characterizes a threat actor?
   A. They are all highly-skilled individuals.
   B. They always use advanced tools to launch attacks.
   C. They always try to cause some harm to an individual or organization.
   D. They all belong to organized crime.

Answer: C.

Question 61:

A computer is presenting a user with a screen requesting payment before the user data is allowed to be accessed by the same user. What type of malware is this?
   A. a type of logic bomb
   B. a type of virus
   C. a type of worm
   D. a type of ransomware

Answer: D.

Explanation
Ransomware commonly encrypts data on a computer and makes the data unavailable until the computer user pays a specific sum of money

Question 62:

Which ICMPv6 message type provides network addressing information to hosts that use SLAAC?

A. router solicitation
B. neighbor advertisement
C. neighbor solicitation
D. router advertisement

Answer: D.

Question 63:
Which tol included in the Security Onion is a series of software plugins that send different types of data to the Elasticsearch data stores?
A. Curator
B. Beats
C. OSSEC
D. ElastAlert

Answer: B.

Question 64:
Which two types of unreadable network traffic could be eliminated from data collected by NSM? (Choose two.)
A. STP traffic
B. IPsec traffic
C. routing updates traffic
D. SSLtraffic
E. broadcast traffic

Answer: B, D.

Explanation
To reduce the huge amount of data collected so that cybersecurity analysts can focus on critical threats, some less important or unusable data could be eliminated from the datasets. For example, encrypted data, such as IPsec and SSL traffic, could be eliminated because it is unreadable in a reasonable time frame.

Question 65:
Which core open source component of the Elastic-stack is responsible for accepting the data in its native format and making elements of the data consistent across all sources?
A. Logstash
B. Kibana
C. Beats
D. Elasticsearch

Answer: D.

Question 66:

In the NIST incident response process life cycle, which type of attack vector involves the use of brute force against devices, networks, or services?

    A. media
    B. impersonation
    C. attrition
    D. loss or theft

Answer: C.

Explanation
Common attack vectors include media, attrition, impersonation, and loss or theft. Attrition attacks are any attacks that use brute force. Media attacks are those initiated from storage devices. Impersonation attacks occur when something or someone is replaced for the purpose of the attack, and loss or theft attacks are initiated by equipment inside the organization.

Question 67:

What is a characteristic of CybOX (Cyber Observable Expression)?

    A. It is a set of standardized schemata for specifying, capturing, characterizing, and communicating events and properties of network operations.
    B. It enables the real-time exchange of cyberthreat indicators between the U.S Federal Government and the private sector.
    C. It is a set of specifications for exchanging cyber threat information between organizations.
    D. It is the specification for an application layer protocol that allows the communication of CTI over HTTPS.

Answer: A.

Question 68:

What are two ways that ICMP can be a security threat to a company? (Choose two.)

    A. by collecting information about a network
    B. by corrupting data between email servers and email recipients
    C. by the infiltration of web pages
    D. by corrupting network IP data packets
    E. by providing a conduit for DoS attacks

Answer: A, E.

Explanation
ICMP can be used as a conduit for DoS attacks. It can be used to collect information about a network such as the identification of hosts and network structure, and by determining the operating systems being used on the network.

Question 69:
Which three IPv4 header fields have no equivalent in an IPv6 header? (Choose three.)
- A. fragment offset
- B. protocol
- C. flag
- D. TTL
- E. Identification
- F. version

Answer: A, C, E.

Explanation
Unlike IPv4, IPv6 routers do not perform fragmentation. Therefore, all three fields supporting fragmentation in the IPv4 header are removed and have no equivalent in the IPv6 header. These three fields are fragment offset, flag, and identification. IPv6 does support host packet fragmentation through the use of extension headers, which are not part of the IPv6 header.

Question 70:
Which two net commands are associated with network resource sharing? (Choose two.)
- A. net start
- B. net accounts
- C. net share
- D. net use
- E. net stop

Answer: C, D.

Explanation
The net command is a very important command. Some common net commands include these:
- **net accounts** – sets password and logon requirements for users
- **net session** – lists or disconnects sessions between a computer and other computers on the network
- **net share** – creates, removes, or manages shared resources
- **net start** – starts a network service or lists running network services
- **net stop** – stops a network service
- **net use** – connects, disconnects, and displays information about shared network resources
- **net view** – shows a list of computers and network devices on the network
- **net session** – lists or disconnects sessions between a computer and other computers on the

Question 71:
Which PDU format is used when bits are received from the network medium by the NIC of a host?

A. segment
B. file
C. packet
D. frame

Answer: D.

Explanation
When received at the physical layer of a host, the bits are formatted into a frame at the data link layer. A packet is the PDU at the network layer. A segment is the PDU at the transport layer. A file is a data structure that may be used at the application layer.

Question 72:
A user is executing a tracert to a remote device. At what point would a router, which is in the path to the destination device, stop forwarding the packet?
   A. when the router receives an ICMP Time Exceeded message
   B. when the values of both the Echo Request and Echo Reply messages reach zero
   C. when the RTT value reaches zero
   D. when the value in the TTL field reaches zero
   E. when the host responds with an ICMP Echo Reply message

Answer: D.

Explanation
When a router receives a traceroute packet, the value in the TTL field is decremented by 1. When the value in the field reaches zero, the receiving router will not forward the packet, and will send an ICMP Time Exceeded message back to the source.

Question 73:
What are two problems that can be caused by a large number of ARP request and reply messages?
   A. All ARP request messages must be processed by all nodes on the local network.
   B. A large number of ARP request and reply messages may slow down the switching process, leading the switch to make many changes in its MAC table.
   C. The network may become overloaded because ARP reply messages have a very large payload due to the 48-bit MAC address and 32-bit IP address that they contain.
   D. The ARP request is sent as a broadcast, and will flood the entire subnet.
   E. Switches become overloaded because they concentrate all the traffic from the attached subnets.

Answer: A, D.

Explanation
(1) All nodes will receive them, and they will be processed by software, interrupting the CPU.

(2) The switch forwards (floods) Layer 2 broadcasts to all ports. A switch does not change its MAC table based on ARP request or reply messages. The switch populates the MAC table using the source MAC address of all frames. The ARP payload is very small and does not overload the switch.

Question 74:
If the default gateway is configured incorrectly on the host, what is the impact on communications?
    A. The host is unable to communicate on the local network.
    B. The host can communicate with other hosts on the local network, but is unable to communicate with hosts on remote networks.
    C. The host can communicate with other hosts on remote networks, but is unable to communicate with hosts on the local network.
    D. There is no impact on communications

Answer: B.

Explanation
A default gateway is only required to communicate with devices on another network. The absence of a default gateway does not affect connectivity between devices on the same local network

Question 75:
When a connectionless protocol is in use at a lower layer of the OSI model, how is missing data detected and retransmitted if necessary?
    A. Connectionless acknowledgements are used to request retransmission
    B. Upper-layer connection-oriented protocols keep track of the data received and can request retransmission from the upper-level protocols on the sending host.
    C. Network layer IP protocols manage the communication sessions if connection-oriented transport services are not available.
    D. The best-effort delivery process guarantees that all packets that are sent are received

Answer: B.

Explanation
When connectionless protocols are in use at a lower layer of the OSI model, upper-level protocols may need to work together on the sending and receiving hosts to account for and retransmit lost data. In some cases, this is not necessary, because for some applications a certain amount of data loss is tolerable.

Question 76:
What is the prefix length notation for the subnet mask 255.255.255.224?
    A. /25
    B. /26

C. /27

D. /28

Answer: C.

Explanation

The binary format for 255.255.255.224 is 11111111.11111111.11111111.11100000. The prefix length is the number of consecutive 1s in the subnet mask. Therefore, the prefix length is /27.

Question 77:

Which network monitoring tool saves captured network frames in PCAP files?
   A. three-way handshake
   B. socket pair
   C. two-way handshake
   D. sliding window

Answer: D.

Explanation

TCP uses windows to attempt to manage the rate of transmission to the maximum flow that the network and destination device can support while minimizing loss and retransmissions. When overwhelmed with data, the destination can send a request to reduce the window. This congestion avoidance is called sliding windows

Question 78:

What is the Internet?
   A. It is a network based on Ethernet technology.
   B. It provides network access for mobile devices.
   C. It provides connections through interconnected global networks.
   D. It is a private network for an organization with LAN and WAN connections.

Answer: C.

Explanation

The Internet provides global connections that enable networked devices (workstations and mobile devices) with different network technologies, such as Ethernet, DSL/cable, and serial connections, to communicate. A private network for an organization with LAN and WAN connections is an intranet.

Question 79:

Which protocol is used by the traceroute command to send and receive echo-requests and echo-replies?
   A. SNMP
   B. ICMP

36

C. Telnet

D. TCP

Answer:

Explanation

Traceroute uses the ICMP (Internet Control Message Protocol) to send and receive echo-request and echo-reply messages.

Question 80:

What are two ICMPv6 messages that are not present in ICMP for IPv4?

A. Neighbor Solicitation

B. Destination Unreachable

C. Host Confirmation

D. Time Exceeded

E. Router Advertisement

F. Route Redirection

Answer: A, E.

Explanation

ICMPv6 includes four new message types: Router Advertisement, Neighbor Advertisement, Router Solicitation, and Neighbor Solicitation.

Question 81:

What are two monitoring tools that capture network traffic and forward it to network monitoring devices?

A. SPAN

B. network tap

C. SNMP

D. SIEM

E. Wireshark

Answer: A, B.

Explanation

A network tap is used to capture traffic for monitoring the network. The tap is typically a passive splitting device implemented inline on the network and forwards all traffic including physical layer errors to an analysis device. SPAN is a port mirroring technology supported on Cisco switches that enables the switch to copy frames and forward them to an analysis device.

Question 82:

Which network monitoring tool is in the category of network protocol analyzers?

A. SNMP

B. SPAN
C. Wireshark
D. SIEM

Answer: C.

Explanation
Wireshark is a network protocol analyzer used to capture network traffic. The traffic captured by Wireshark is saved in PCAP files and includes interface information and timestamps

Question 83:
What are three benefits of using symbolic links over hard links in Linux? (Choose three.)
   A. They can link to a directory.
   B. They can be compressed.
   C. Symbolic links can be exported.
   D. They can be encrypted.
   E. They can link to a file in a different file system.
   F. They can show the location of the original file.

Answer: A, E, F.

Explanation
In Linux, a hard link is another file that points to the same location as the original file. A soft link (also called a symbolic link or a symlink) is a link to another file system name. Hard links are limited to the file system in which they are created and they cannot link to a directory; soft links are not limited to the same file system and they can link to a directory. To see the location of the original file for a symbolic link use the ls –l command.

Question 84:
A network security specialist is tasked to implement a security measure that monitors the status of critical files in the data center and sends an immediate alert if any file is modified. Which aspect of secure communications is addressed by this security measure?
   A. origin authentication
   B. data integrity
   C. nonrepudiation
   D. data confidentiality

Answer: B.

Explanation
Secure communications consists of four elements:
   • Data confidentiality – guarantees that only authorized users can read the message
   • Data integrity – guarantees that the message was not altered

- Origin authentication – guarantees that the message is not a forgery and does actually come from whom it states
- Data nonrepudiation – guarantees that the sender cannot repudiate, or refute, the validity of a message sent

Question 85:
A network administrator is configuring an AAA server to manage TACACS+ authentication. What are two attributes of TACACS+ authentication? (Choose two.)
   A. TCP port 40
   B. encryption for all communication
   C. single process for authentication and authorization
   D. UDP port 1645
   E. encryption for only the password of a user
   F. separate processes for authentication and authorization

Answer: B, F.

Explanation
TACACS+ authentication includes the following attributes: Separates authentication and authorization processes Encrypts all communication, not just passwords Utilizes TCP port 49

Question 86:
In an attempt to prevent network attacks, cyber analysts share unique identifiable attributes of known attacks with colleagues. What three types of attributes or indicators of compromise are helpful to share? (Choose three.)
   A. IP addresses of attack servers
   B. changes made to end system software
   C. netbios names of compromised firewalls
   D. features of malware files
   E. BIOS of attacking systems
   F. system ID of compromised systems

Answer: A, B, D.

Explanation
Many network attacks can be prevented by sharing information about indicators of compromise (IOC). Each attack has unique identifiable attributes. Indicators of compromise are the evidence that an attack has occurred. IOCs can be identifying features of malware files, IP addresses of servers that are used in the attack, filenames, and characteristic changes made to end system software.

Question 87:
Which two types of messages are used in place of ARP for address resolution in IPv6? (Choose two.)

A. anycast
B. broadcast
C. neighbor solicitation
D. echo reply
E. echo request
F. neighbor advertisement

Answer: C, F.

Explanation
IPv6 does not use ARP. Instead, ICMPv6 neighbor discovery is used by sending neighbor solicitation and neighbor advertisement messages.

Question 88:
What is indicated by a true negative security alert classification?
A. An alert is verified to be an actual security incident.
B. An alert is incorrectly issued and does not indicate an actual security incident.
C. Normal traffic is correctly ignored and erroneous alerts are not being issued.
D. Exploits are not being detected by the security systems that are in place.

Answer: C.

Explanation
True negative classifications are desirable because they indicate that normal traffic is correctly not being identified as malicious traffic by security measures.

Question 89:
Which statement describes the anomaly-based intrusion detection approach?
A. It compares the antivirus definition file to a cloud based repository for latest updates.
B. It compares the behavior of a host to an established baseline to identify potential intrusions.
C. It compares the signatures of incoming traffic to a known intrusion database.
D. It compares the operations of a host against a well-defined security policy.

Answer: B.

Explanation
With an anomaly-based intrusion detection approach, a baseline of host behaviors is established first. The host behavior is checked against the baseline to detect significant deviations, which might indicate potential intrusions.

Question 90:
Which two protocols are associated with the transport layer? (Choose two.)
A. ICMP

B. IP
C. UDP
D. PPP
E. TCP

Answer: C, E.

Explanation
TCP and UDP reside at the transport layer in both the OSI and TCP/IP models.

Question 91:
A network administrator is creating a network profile to generate a network baseline.
What is included in the critical asset address space element?
  A. the time between the establishment of a data flow and its termination
  B. the TCP and UDP daemons and ports that are allowed to be open on the server
  C. the IP addresses or the logical location of essential systems or data
  D. the list of TCP or UDP processes that are available to accept data

Answer: C.

Explanation
A network profile should include some important elements, such as the following:
  • Total throughput – the amount of data passing from a given source to a given destination in a given period of time
  • Session duration – the time between the establishment of a data flow and its termination
  • Ports used – a list of TCP or UDP processes that are available to accept data
  • Critical asset address space – the IP addresses or the logical location of essential systems or data

Question 92:
What are the three impact metrics contained in the CVSS 3.0 Base Metric Group?
(Choose three.)
  A. confidentiality
  B. remediation level
  C. integrity
  D. attack vector
  E. exploit
  F. availability

Answer: A, C, F.

Explanation
The Common Vulnerability Scoring System (CVSS) is a vendor-neutral, industry standard, open framework for weighing the risks of a vulnerability using a variety of metrics. CVSS uses three

groups of metrics to assess vulnerability, the Base Metric Group, Temporal Metric Group, and Environmental Metric Group.

The Base Metric Group has two classes of metrics (exploitability and impact). The impact metrics are rooted in the following areas: confidentiality, integrity, and availability.

Question 93:
What is a characteristic of DNS?
    A. DNS servers can cache recent queries to reduce DNS query traffic.
    B. All DNS servers must maintain mappings for the entire DNS structure.
    C. DNS servers are programmed to drop requests for name translations that are not within their zone.
    D. DNS relies on a hub-and-spoke topology with centralized servers.

Answer: A.

Explanation
DNS uses a hierarchy for decentralized servers to perform name resolution. DNS servers only maintain records for their zone and can cache recent queries so that future queries do not produce excessive DNS traffic.

Question 94:
What are the two differences between HTTP and HTTP/2? (Choose two.)
    A. HTTP/2 uses a compressed header to reduce bandwidth requirements.
    B. HTTP/2 uses multiplexing to support multiple streams and enhance efficiency.
    C. HTTP/2 uses different status codes than HTTP does to improve performance.
    D. HTTP/2 issues requests using a text format whereas HTTP uses binary commands.
    E. HTTP has a different header format than HTTP/2 has.

Answer: A, B.

Explanation
The purpose of HTTP/2 is to improve HTTP performance by addressing the latency issues of HTTP. This is accomplished using features such as multiplexing, server push, binary code, and header compression.

Question 95:
Which two statements describe access attacks? (Choose two.)
    A. Password attacks can be implemented by the use of brute-force attack methods, Trojan horses, or packet sniffers.
    B. To detect listening services, port scanning attacks scan a range of TCP or UDP port numbers on a host.
    C. Port redirection attacks use a network adapter card in promiscuous mode to capture all network packets that are sent across a LAN.

D. Trust exploitation attacks often involve the use of a laptop to act as a rogue access point to capture and copy all network traffic in a public location, such as a wireless hotspot.

E. Buffer overflow attacks write data beyond the allocated buffer memory to overwrite valid data or to exploit systems to execute malicious code.

Answer: A, E.

Explanation
An access attack tries to gain access to a resource using a hijacked account or other means. The five types of access attacks include the following:

- **password** – a dictionary is used for repeated login attempts

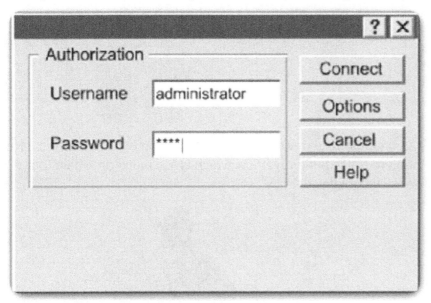

- **trust exploitation** – uses granted privileges to access unauthorized material

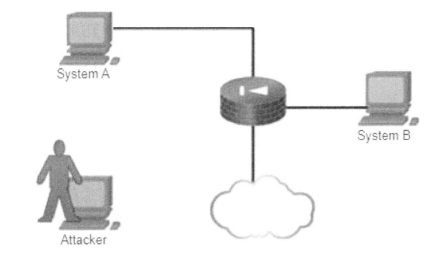

- **port redirection** – uses a compromised internal host to pass traffic through a firewall

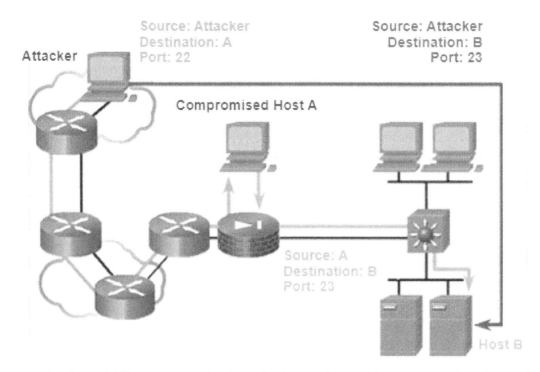

Source: Attacker
Destination: A
Port: 22

Source: Attacker
Destination: B
Port: 23

Attacker

Compromised Host A

Source: A
Destination: B
Port: 23

Host B

- **man-in-the-middle** – an unauthorized device positioned between two legitimate devices in order to redirect or capture traffic buffer overflow which is too much data sent to a memory location that already contains data.

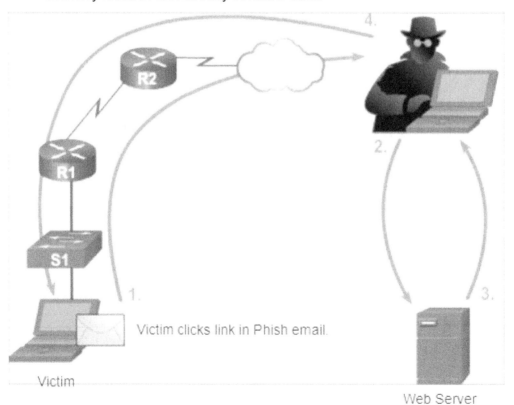

Victim clicks link in Phish email.

Victim

Web Server

Chapter 3: 200-201 CBROPS Mock Test #2

Question 1:
For what purpose would a network administrator use the Nmap tool?
   A. protection of the private IP addresses of internal hosts
   B. identification of specific network anomalies
   C. collection and analysis of security alerts and logs
   D. detection and identification of open ports

Answer: D.

Question 2:
What network attack seeks to create a DoS for clients by preventing them from being able to obtain a DHCP lease?
   A. DHCP starvation
   B. IP address spoofing
   C. DHCP spoofing
   D. CAM table attack

Answer: A.

Explanation
The DHCP starvation attacks are launched by an attacker with the intent to create a DoS for DHCP clients. To accomplish this goal, the attacker uses a tool that sends many DHCPDISCOVER messages in order to lease the entire pool of available IP addresses, thus denying them to legitimate hosts.

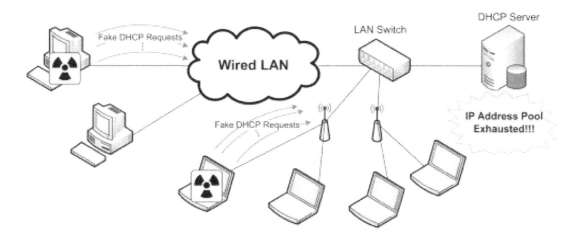

Question 3:
A company has a file server that shares a folder named Public. The network security policy specifies that the Public folder is assigned Read-Only rights to anyone who can

log into the server while the Edit rights are assigned only to the network admin group. Which component is addressed in the AAA network service framework?
   A. automation
   B. authentication
   C. authorization
   D. accounting

Answer: C.

Explanation
After a user is successfully authenticated (logged into the server), the authorization is the process of determining what network resources the user can access and what operations (such as read or edit) the user can perform.

Question 4:
A person coming to a cafe for the first time wants to gain wireless access to the Internet using a laptop. What is the first step the wireless client will do in order to communicate over the network using a wireless management frame?
   A. associate with the AP
   B. authenticate to the AP
   C. discover the AP
   D. agree with the AP on the payload

Answer: C.

Explanation
In order for wireless devices to communicate on a wireless network, management frames are used to complete a three-stage process: Discover the AP Authenticate with the AP Associate with the AP

Question 5:
A device has been assigned the IPv6 address of 2001:0db8:cafe:4500:1000:00d8:0058:00ab/64. Which is the network identifier of the device?
   A. 2001:0db8:cafe:4500:1000
   B. 2001:0db8:cafe:4500:1000:0058:00ab
   C. 1000:00d8:0058:00ab
   D. 2001:0db8:cafe:4500
   E. 2001

Answer: D.

Explanation

The address has a prefix length of /64. Thus the first 64 bits represent the network portion, whereas the last 64 bits represent the host portion of the IPv6 address.

Question 6:

An administrator wants to create four subnetworks from the network address 192.168.1.0/24. What is the network address and subnet mask of the second usable subnet?

    A. subnetwork 192.168.1.64 subnet mask 255.255.255.192
    B. subnetwork 192.168.1.64 subnet mask 255.255.255.240
    C. subnetwork 192.168.1.32 subnet mask 255.255.255.240
    D. subnetwork 192.168.1.128 subnet mask 255.255.255.192
    E. subnetwork 192.168.1.8 subnet mask 255.255.255.224

Answer:

Question 7:

What term describes a set of software tools designed to increase the privileges of a user or to grant access to the user to portions of the operating system that should not normally be allowed?

    A. compiler
    B. rootkit
    C. package manager
    D. penetration testing

Answer: B.

Explanation
A rootkit is used by an attacker to secure a backdoor to a compromised computer, grant access to portions of the operating system normally not permitted, or increase the privileges of a user.

Question 8:

The IT security personnel of an organization notice that the web server deployed in the DMZ is frequently targeted by threat actors. The decision is made to implement a patch management system to manage the server. Which risk management strategy method is being used to respond to the identified risk?

    A. risk sharing
    B. risk avoidance
    C. risk reduction
    D. risk retention

Answer: C.

Explanation
There are four potential strategies for responding to risks that have been identified:

- **Risk avoidance** – Stop performing the activities that create risk.
- **Risk reduction** – Decrease the risk by taking measures to reduce vulnerability.
- **Risk sharing** – Shift some of the risk to other parties.
- **Risk retention** – Accept the risk and its consequences.

Question 9:

What are three characteristics of an information security management system? (Choose three.)

    A. It involves the implementation of systems that track the location and configuration of networked devices and software across an enterprise.

    B. It is a systematic and multilayered approach to cybersecurity.

    C. It addresses the inventory and control of hardware and software configurations of systems.

    D. It consists of a set of practices that are systematically applied to ensure continuous improvement in information security.

    E. It consists of a management framework through which an organization identifies, analyzes, and addresses information security risks.

    F. It is based on the application of servers and security devices.

Answer: B, D, E.

Explanation
An Information Security Management System (ISMS) consists of a management framework through which an organization identifies, analyzes, and addresses information security risks. ISMSs are not based on servers or security devices. Instead, an ISMS consists of a set of practices that are systematically applied by an organization to ensure continuous improvement in information security.

ISMSs provide conceptual models that guide organizations in planning, implementing, governing, and evaluating information security programs. ISMSs are a natural extension of the use of popular business models, such as Total Quality Management (TQM) and Control Objectives for Information and Related Technologies (COBIT), into the realm of cybersecurity. An ISMS is a systematic, multi-layered approach to cybersecurity. The approach includes people, processes, technologies, and the cultures in which they interact in a process of risk management.

Question 10:

Which three technologies should be included in a SOC security information and event management system? (Choose three.)

    A. event collection, correlation, and analysis

    B. security monitoring

    C. user authentication

    D. proxy service

    E. intrusion prevention

    F. threat intelligence

Answer: A, B, F.

Explanation

Technologies in a SOC should include the following:

- Event collection, correlation, and analysis
- Security monitoring
- Security control
- Log management
- Vulnerability assessment
- Vulnerability tracking
- Threat intelligence Proxy server, VPN, and IPS are security devices deployed in the network infrastructure.

Question 11:

What part of the URL, http://www.cisco.com/index.html, represents the top-level DNS domain?

    A. http

    B. www

    C. .com

    D. index

Answer: C.

Explanation

The components of the URL http://www.cisco.com/index.htm are as follows:

http = protocol www = part of the server name cisco = part of the domain name index = file name com = the top-level domain

Question 12:

What best describes the security threat of spoofing?

    A. sending bulk email to individuals, lists, or domains with the intention to prevent users from accessing email

    B. sending abnormally large amounts of data to a remote server to prevent user access to the server services

    C. intercepting traffic between two hosts or inserting false information into traffic between two hosts

    D. making data appear to come from a source that is not the actual source

Answer: D.

Question 13:

A newly created company has fifteen Windows 10 computers that need to be installed before the company can open for business. What is a best practice that the technician should implement when configuring the Windows Firewall?

    A. The technician should remove all default firewall rules and selectively deny traffic from reaching the company network.

    B. After implementing third party security software for the company, the technician should verify that the Windows Firewall is disabled.

    C. The technician should create instructions for corporate users on how to allow an app through the Windows Firewall using the Administrator account.

    D. The technician should enable the Windows Firewall for inbound traffic and install other firewall software for outbound traffic control.

Answer: B.

Explanation
Only disable Windows Firewall if other firewall software is installed. Use the Windows Firewall (Windows 7 or 8) or the Windows Defender Firewall (Windows 10) Control Panel to enable or disable the Windows Firewall.

Question 14:
Which statement defines the difference between session data and transaction data in logs?

    A. Session data analyzes network traffic and predicts network behavior, whereas transaction data records network sessions.

    B. Session data is used to make predictions on network behaviors, whereas transaction data is used to detect network anomalies.

    C. Session data records a conversation between hosts, whereas transaction data focuses on the result of network sessions.

    D. Session data shows the result of a network session, whereas transaction data is in response to network threat traffic.

Answer: C.

Question 15:
Which device supports the use of SPAN to enable monitoring of malicious activity?

    A. Cisco Catalyst switch

    B. Cisco IronPort

    C. Cisco NAC

    D. Cisco Security Agent

Answer: A.

Explanation

SPAN is a Cisco technology that allows all of the traffic from one port to be redirected to another port.

Question 16:

Which term is used for describing automated queries that are useful for adding efficiency to the cyberoperations workflow?

    A. cyber kill chain
    B. playbook
    C. chain of custody
    D. rootkit

Answer: B.

Explanation
A playbook is an automated query that can add efficiency to the cyberoperations workflow.

Question 17:

When ACLs are configured to block IP address spoofing and DoS flood attacks, which ICMP message should be allowed both inbound and outbound?

    A. echo reply
    B. unreachable
    C. source quench
    D. echo

Answer: D.

Question 18:

After a security monitoring tool identifies a malware attachment entering the network, what is the benefit of performing a retrospective analysis?

    A. It can identify how the malware originally entered the network.
    B. A retrospective analysis can help in tracking the behavior of the malware from the identification point forward.
    C. It can calculate the probability of a future incident.
    D. It can determine which network host was first affected.

Answer: B.

Explanation
General security monitoring can identify when a malware attachment enters a network and which host is first infected. Retrospective analysis takes the next step and is the tracking of the behavior of the malware from that point forward.

Question 19:

Which two data types would be classified as personally identifiable information (PII)? (Choose two.)

    A. house thermostat reading

    B. average number of cattle per region

    C. vehicle identification number

    D. hospital emergency use per region

    E. Facebook photographs

Answer: C, E.

Question 20:

A help desk technician notices an increased number of calls relating to the performance of computers located at the manufacturing plant. The technician believes that botnets are causing the issue. What are the two purposes of botnets? (Choose two.)

    A. to transmit viruses or spam to computers on the same network

    B. to record any and all keystrokes

    C. to attack other computers

    D. to withhold access to a computer or files until money has been paid

    E. to gain access to the restricted part of the operating system

Answer: A, C.

Explanation
Botnets can be used to perform DDoS attacks, obtain data, or transmit malware to other devices on the network.

Question 21:

Which meta-feature element in the Diamond Model classifies the general type of intrusion event?

    A. phase

    B. results

    C. methodology

    D. direction

Answer: C.

Explanation
Methodology – This is used to classify the general type of event, such as port scan, phishing, content delivery attack, syn flood, etc.

Question 22:

Which Linux command is used to manage processes?

    A. chrootkit

    B. ls

C. grep
D. kill

Answer: D.

Explanation
The kill command is used to stop, restart, or pause a process. The chrootkit command is used to check the computer for rootkits, a set of software tools that can increase the privilege level of a user or grant access to portions of software normally not allowed. The grep command is used to look for a file or text within a file. The ls command is used to list files, directories, and file information.

Question 23:
What Cisco management system is used to analyze application analysis data into dashboard reports?
   A. NetFlow
   B. NBAR2
   C. Prime
   D. IPFIX

Answer: C.

Explanation
A management and reporting system, such as Cisco Prime, can be used to analyze and present the application analysis data into dashboard reports for use by network monitoring personnel.

Question 24:
Which Windows Event Viewer log includes events regarding the operation of drivers, processes, and hardware?
   A. system logs
   B. application logs
   C. security logs
   D. setup logs

Answer: A.

Explanation
By default Windows keeps four types of host logs:
   - **Application logs** – events logged by various applications
   - **System logs** – events about the operation of drivers, processes, and hardware
   - **Setup logs** – information about the installation of software, including Windows updates
   - **Security logs** – events related to security, such as logon attempts and operations related to file or object management and access

Question 25:

Which method is used to make data unreadable to unauthorized users?

    A. Encrypt the data.

    B. Fragment the data.

    C. Add a checksum to the end of the data.

    D. Assign it a username and password.

Answer: A.

Explanation

Network data can be encrypted using various cryptography applications so that the data is made unreadable to unauthorized users. Authorized users have the cryptography application so the data can be unencrypted.

Question 26:

For network systems, which management system addresses the inventory and control of hardware and software configurations?

    A. asset management

    B. vulnerability management

    C. risk management

    D. configuration management

Answer: D.

Explanation

Configuration management addresses the inventory and control of hardware and software configurations of network systems.

Question 27:
What are the three core functions provided by the Security Onion? (Choose three.)
- A. business continuity planning
- B. full packet capture
- C. alert analysis
- D. intrusion detection
- E. security device management
- F. threat containment

Answer: B, C, D.

Explanation
Security Onion is an open source suite of Network Security Monitoring (NSM) tools for evaluating cybersecurity alerts. For cybersecurity analysts the Security Onion provides full packet capture, network-based and host-based intrusion detection systems, and alert analysis tools.

Question 28:
In NAT terms, what address type refers to the globally routable IPv4 address of a destination host on the Internet?
- A. outside global
- B. inside global
- C. outside local
- D. inside local

Answer: A.

Explanation
From the perspective of a NAT device, inside global addresses are used by external users to reach internal hosts. Inside local addresses are the addresses assigned to internal hosts. Outside global addresses are the addresses of destinations on the external network. Outside local addresses are the actual private addresses of destination hosts behind other NAT devices.

Question 29:
Which two fields or features does Ethernet examine to determine if a received frame is passed to the data link layer or discarded by the NIC? (Choose two.)
- A. CEF
- B. source MAC address
- C. minimum frame size
- D. auto-MDIX
- E. Frame Check Sequence

Answer: C, E.

Question 30:
Which type of data would be considered an example of volatile data?
    A. web browser cache
    B. memory registers
    C. log files
    D. temp files

Answer: B.

Explanation
Volatile data is data stored in memory such as registers, cache, and RAM, or it is data that exists in transit. Volatile memory is lost when the computer loses power.

Question 31:
What is the main purpose of exploitations by a threat actor through the weapon delivered to a target during the Cyber Kill Chain exploitation phase?
    A. Launch a DoS attack.
    B. Send a message back to a CnC controlled by the threat actor.
    C. Break the vulnerability and gain control of the target.
    D. Establish a backdoor into the system.

Answer: C.

Explanation
After the weapon has been delivered, the threat actor uses it to break the vulnerability and gain control of the target. The threat actor will use an exploit that gains the effect desired, does it quietly, and avoids detections. Establishing a back door in the target system is the phase of installation.

Question 32:
What three security tools does Cisco Talos maintain security incident detection rule sets for? (Choose three.)
    A. Snort
    B. NetStumbler
    C. Socat
    D. SpamCop
    E. ClamAV

Answer: A, D, E.

Question 33:

Which host-based firewall uses a three-profile approach to configure the firewall functionality?
   A. Windows Firewall
   B. iptables
   C. TCP Wrapper
   D. nftables

Answer: A.

Explanation
Windows Firewall uses a profile-based approach to configuring firewall functionality. It uses three profiles, Public, Private, and Domain, to define firewall functions.

Question 34:
When a user visits an online store website that uses HTTPS, the user browser queries the CA for a CRL. What is the purpose of this query?
   A. to verify the validity of the digital certificate
   B. to request the CA self-signed digital certificate
   C. to check the length of key used for the digital certificate
   D. to negotiate the best encryption to use

Answer: A.

Explanation
A digital certificate must be revoked if it is invalid. CAs maintain a certificate revocation list (CRL), a list of revoked certificate serial numbers that have been invalidated. The user browser will query the CRL to verify the validity of a certificate.

Question 35:
Which step in the Vulnerability Management Life Cycle determines a baseline risk profile to eliminate risks based on asset criticality, vulnerability threat, and asset classification?
   A. discover
   B. assess
   C. prioritize assets
   D. verify

Answer: B.

Explanation
The steps in the Vulnerability Management Life Cycle include these:
   • **Discover** – inventory all assets across the network and identify host details, including operating systems and open services, to identify vulnerabilities
   • **Prioritize assets** – categorize assets into groups or business units, and assign a business value to asset groups based on their criticality to business operations

- **Assess** – determine a baseline risk profile to eliminate risks based on asset criticality, vulnerability threats, and asset classification
- **Report** – measure the level of business risk associated with assets according to security policies. Document a security plan, monitor suspicious activity, and describe known vulnerabilities.
- **Remediate** – prioritize according to business risk and fix vulnerabilities in order of risk
- **Verify** – verity that threats have been eliminated through follow-up audits

Question 36:

Which management system implements systems that track the location and configuration of networked devices and software across an enterprise?

    A. asset management

    B. vulnerability management

    C. risk management

    D. configuration management

Answer: A.

Explanation

Asset management involves the implementation of systems that track the location and configuration of networked devices and software across an enterprise.

Question 37:

A network administrator is reviewing server alerts because of reports of network slowness. The administrator confirms that an alert was an actual security incident. What is the security alert classification of this type of scenario?
  A. false negative
  B. true positive
  C. true negative
  D. false positive

Answer: B.

Question 38:

Which application layer protocol is used to provide file-sharing and print services to Microsoft applications?
  A. SMTP
  B. HTTP
  C. SMB
  D. DHCP

Answer: C.

Explanation
SMB is used in Microsoft networking for file-sharing and print services. The Linux operating system provides a method of sharing resources with Microsoft networks by using a version of SMB called SAMBA.

Question 39:

Which device in a layered defense-in-depth approach denies connections initiated from untrusted networks to internal networks, but allows internal users within an organization to connect to untrusted networks?
  A. access layer switch
  B. firewall
  C. internal router
  D. IPS

Answer: B.

Explanation
A firewall is typically a second line of defense in a layered defense-in-depth approach to network security. The firewall typically connects to an edge router that connects to the service provider. The firewall tracks connections initiated within the company going out of the company

and denies initiation of connections from external untrusted networks going to internal trusted networks.

Question 40:
Which three procedures in Sguil are provided to security analysts to address alerts? (Choose three.)
- A. Escalate an uncertain alert.
- B. Correlate similar alerts into a single line.
- C. Categorize true positives.
- D. Pivot to other information sources and tools.
- E. Construct queries using Query Builder.
- F. Expire false positives.

Answer: A, C, F.

Explanation
Sguil is a tool for addressing alerts. Three tasks can be completed in Sguil to manage alerts: Alerts that have been found to be false positives can be expired. An alert can be escalated if the cybersecurity analyst is uncertain how to handle it. Events that have been identified as true positives can be categorized.

Question 41:
Which two services are provided by the NetFlow tool? (Choose two.)
- A. QoS configuration
- B. usage-based network billing
- C. log analysis
- D. access list monitoring
- E. network monitoring

Answer: B, E.

Explanation
NetFlow efficiently provides an important set of services for IP applications including network traffic accounting, usage-based network billing, network planning, security, denial of service monitoring capabilities, and network monitoring.

Question 42:
An administrator discovers that a user is accessing a newly established website that may be detrimental to company security. What action should the administrator take first in terms of the security policy?
- A. Ask the user to stop immediately and inform the user that this constitutes grounds for dismissal.
- B. Create a firewall rule blocking the respective website.
- C. Revise the AUP immediately and get all users to sign the updated

D. Immediately suspend the network privileges of the user.

Answer: C.

Question 43:
Which two tasks can be performed by a local DNS server? (Choose two.)
  A. allowing data transfer between two network devices
  B. retrieving email messages
  C. providing IP addresses to local hosts
  D. forwarding name resolution requests between servers
  E. mapping name-to-IP addresses for internal hosts

Answer: D, E.

Question 44:
Which type of event is logged in Cisco Next-Generation IPS devices (NGIPS) using FirePOWER Services when changes have been detected in the monitored network?
  A. intrusion
  B. connection
  C. host or endpoint
  D. network discovery

Answer: D.

Explanation
Network discovery events in Cisco NGIPS represent changes that have been detected in the monitored network.

Question 45:
Which statement describes the state of the administrator and guest accounts after a user installs Windows desktop version to a new computer?
  A. By default, the guest account is enabled but the administrator account is disabled.
  B. By default, both the administrator and guest accounts are enabled.
  C. By default, both the administrator and guest accounts are disabled.
  D. By default, the administrator account is enabled but the guest account is disabled.

Answer: C.

Explanation
When a user installs Windows desktop version, two local user accounts are created automatically during the process, administrator and guest. Both accounts are disabled by default.

Question 46:

What subnet mask is represented by the slash notation /20?
   A. 255.255.255.0
   B. 255.255.255.248
   C. 255.255.255.192
   D. 255.255.240.0
   E. 255.255.224.0

Answer: D.

Explanation
The slash notation /20 represents a subnet mask with 20 1s. This would translate to: 11111111.11111111.11110000.0000, which in turn would convert into 255.255.240.0.

Question 47:
What is the benefit of converting log file data into a common schema?
   A. creates a data model based on fields of data from a source
   B. creates a set of regex-based field extractions
   C. allows the implementation of partial normalization and inspection
   D. allows easy processing and analysis of datasets

Answer: D.

Explanation
When data is converted into a universal format, it can be effectively structured for performing fast queries and event analysis.

Question 48:
Which Cisco sponsored certification is designed to provide the first step in acquiring the knowledge and skills to work with a SOC team?
   A. CCNA CyberOps Associate
   B. CCNA Cloud
   C. CCNA Security
   D. CCNA Data Center

Answer: A.

Question 49:
Which three IP addresses are considered private addresses? (Choose three.)
   A. 198.168.6.18
   B. 192.168.5.29
   C. 172.68.83.35
   D. 128.37.255.6
   E. 172.17.254.4
   F. 10.234.2.1

Answer: B, E, F.

Explanation
The designated private IP addresses are within the three IP address ranges:
10.0.0.0 – 10.255.255.255 172.16.0.0 – 172.31.255.255 192.168.0.0 – 192.168.255.255

Question 50:
When establishing a network profile for an organization, which element describes the time between the establishment of a data flow and its termination?
    A. bandwidth of the Internet connection
    B. routing protocol convergence
    C. session duration
    D. total throughput

Answer: C.

Explanation
A network profile should include some important elements, such as the following:
Total throughput – the amount of data passing from a given source to a given destination in a given period of time
Session duration – the time between the establishment of a data flow and its termination
Ports used – a list of TCP or UDP processes that are available to accept data
Critical asset address space – the IP addresses or the logical location of essential systems or data

Question 51:
What are the stages that a wireless device completes before it can communicate over a wireless LAN network?
    A. discover a wireless AP, authenticate with the AP, associate with the AP
    B. discover a wireless AP, associate with the AP, authorize with the AP
    C. discover a wireless AP, associate with the AP, authenticate with the AP
    D. discover a wireless AP, authorize with the AP, associate with the AP

Answer: A.

Question 52:
What are two properties of a cryptographic hash function? (Choose two.)
    A. Complex inputs will produce complex hashes.
    B. The output is a fixed length.
    C. The hash function is one way and irreversible.
    D. Hash functions can be duplicated for authentication purposes.
    E. The input for a particular hash algorithm has to have a fixed size.

Answer: B, C.

Question 53:
Which type of evidence cannot prove an IT security fact on its own?
  A. hearsay
  B. corroborative
  C. best
  D. indirect

Answer: D.

Explanation
Indirect evidence cannot prove a fact on its own, but direct evidence can. Corroborative evidence is supporting information. Best evidence is most reliable because it is something concrete such as a signed contract.

Question 54:
What is a characteristic of a probabilistic analysis in an alert evaluation?
  A. each event an inevitable result of antecedent causes
  B. precise methods that yield the same result every time by relying on predefined conditions
  C. random variables that create difficulty in knowing the outcome of any given event with certainty
  D. analysis of applications that conform to application/networking standards

Answer: A.

Question 55:
Which statement is correct about network protocols?
  A. They define how messages are exchanged between the source and the destination.
  B. They all function in the network access layer of TCP/IP.
  C. They are only required for exchange of messages between devices on remote networks.
  D. Network protocols define the type of hardware that is used and how it is mounted in racks.

Answer: A.

Explanation
Network protocols are implemented in hardware, or software, or both. They interact with each other within different layers of a protocol stack. Protocols have nothing to do with the installation of the network equipment. Network protocols are required to exchange information between source and destination devices in both local and remote networks.

Question 56:

A technician needs to verify file permissions on a specific Linux file. Which command would the technician use?

    A. cd
    B. sudo
    C. ls-l
    D. vi

Answer: C.

Question 57:
Which two protocols may devices use in the application process that sends email? (Choose two.)

    A. HTTP
    B. POP
    C. POP3
    D. DNS
    E. IMAP
    F. SMTP

Answer: D, F.

Explanation
POP, POP3, and IMAP are protocols that are used to retrieve email from servers. SMTP is the default protocol that is used to send email. DNS may be used by the sender email server to find the address of the destination email server. HTTP is a protocol for sending and receiving web pages.

Question 58:
Which file system type was specifically created for optical disk media?

    A. ext3
    B. HFS+
    C. CDFS
    D. ext2

Answer: C.

Question 59:
A piece of malware has gained access to a workstation and issued a DNS lookup query to a CnC server. What is the purpose of this attack?

    A. to check the domain name of the workstation
    B. to send stolen sensitive data with encoding
    C. to masquerade the IP address of the workstation
    D. to request a change of the IP address

Answer: B.

Explanation
A piece of malware, after accessing a host, may exploit the DNS service by communicating with command-and-control (CnC) servers and then exfiltrate data in traffic disguised as normal DNS lookup queries. Various types of encoding, such as base64, 8-bit binary, and hex can be used to camouflage the data and evade basic data loss prevention (DLP) measures.

Question 60:
According to information outlined by the Cyber Kill Chain, which two approaches can help identify reconnaissance threats? (Choose two.)
  A. Analyze web log alerts and historical search data.
  B. Audit endpoints to forensically determine origin of exploit.
  C. Build playbooks for detecting browser behavior.
  D. Conduct full malware analysis.
  E. Understand targeted servers, people, and data available to attack.

Answer: A, C.

Explanation
Threat actors may use port scanning toward a web server of an organization and identify vulnerabilities on the server. They may visit the web server to collect information about the organization. The web server logging should be enabled and the logging data should be analyzed to identify possible reconnaissance threats. Building playbooks by filtering and combining related web activities by visitors can sometimes reveal the intentions of threat actors.

Question 61:
Which two ICMPv6 messages are used during the Ethernet MAC address resolution process? (Choose two.)
  A. router solicitation
  B. router advertisement
  C. neighbor solicitation
  D. neighbor advertisement
  E. echo request

Answer: C, D.

Explanation
IPv6 uses neighbor solicitation (NS) and neighbor advertisement (NA) ICMPv6 messages for MAC address resolution

Question 62:
What best describes the destination IPv4 address that is used by multicasting?
  A. a single IP multicast address that is used by all destinations in a group

B. an IP address that is unique for each destination in the group

C. a group address that shares the last 23 bits with the source IPv4 address

D. a 48 bit address that is determined by the number of members in the multicast group

Answer: A.

Explanation

The destination multicast IPv4 address is a group address, which is a single IP multicast address within the Class D range.

Question 63:

What is the result of using security devices that include HTTPS decryption and inspection services?

A. The devices require continuous monitoring and fine tuning.

B. The devices introduce processing delays and privacy issues.

C. The devices must have preconfigured usernames and passwords for all users.

D. Monthly service contracts with reputable web filtering sites can be costly.

Answer: B.

Explanation

HTTPS adds extra overhead to the HTTP-formed packet. HTTPS encrypts using Secure Sockets Layer (SSL). Even though some devices can perform SSL decryption and inspection, this can present processing and privacy issues.

Question 64:

What is a disadvantage of DDNS?

A. DDNS is considered malignant and must be monitored by security software.

B. DDNS is unable to co-exist on a network subdomain that also uses DNS.

C. Using free DDNS services, threat actors can quickly and easily generate subdomains and change DNS records.

D. Using DDNS, a change in an existing IP address mapping can take over 24 hours and could result in a disruption of connectivity.

Answer: C.

Question 65:

A threat actor has identified the potential vulnerability of the web server of an organization and is building an attack. What will the threat actor possibly do to build an attack weapon?

A. Obtain an automated tool in order to deliver the malware payload through the vulnerability.

B. Install a webshell on the web server for persistent access.

C. Create a point of persistence by adding services.

D. Collect credentials of the web server developers and administrators.

Answer: A.

Explanation
One tactic of weaponization used by a threat actor after the vulnerability is identified is to obtain an automated tool to deliver the malware payload through the vulnerability.

Question 66:
Which tool included in the Security Onion is a series of software plugins that send different types of data to the Elasticsearch data stores?
   A. OSSEC
   B. Curator
   C. Beats
   D. ElastAlert

Answer: C.

Question 67:
Which two statements describe the use of asymmetric algorithms? (Choose two.)
   A. Public and private keys may be used interchangeably.
   B. If a public key is used to encrypt the data, a private key must be used to decrypt the data.
   C. If a public key is used to encrypt the data, a public key must be used to decrypt the data.
   D. If a private key is used to encrypt the data, a public key must be used to decrypt the data.
   E. If a private key is used to encrypt the data, a private key must be used to decrypt the data.

Answer: B, D.

Explanation
Asymmetric algorithms use two keys: a public key and a private key. Both keys are capable of the encryption process, but the complementary matched key is required for decryption. If a public key encrypts the data, the matching private key decrypts the data. The opposite is also true. If a private key encrypts the data, the corresponding public key decrypts the data.

Question 68:
Which three security services are provided by digital signatures? (Choose three.)
   A. provides nonrepudiation using HMAC functions
   B. guarantees data has not changed in transit
   C. provides data encryption
   D. authenticates the source
   E. provides confidentiality of digitally signed data

F. authenticates the destination

Answer: B, C, D.

Explanation
Digital signatures are a mathematical technique used to provide three basic security services. Digital signatures have specific properties that enable entity authentication and data integrity. In addition, digital signatures provide nonrepudiation of the transaction. In other words, the digital signature serves as legal proof that the data exchange did take place.

Question 69:
What are two methods to maintain certificate revocation status? (Choose two.)
  A. CRL
  B. DNS
  C. subordinate CA
  D. OCSP
  E. LDAP

Answer: A, D.

Explanation
A digital certificate might need to be revoked if its key is compromised or it is no longer needed. The certificate revocation list (CRL) and Online Certificate Status Protocol (OCSP), are two common methods to check a certificate revocation status.

Question 70:
What are two uses of an access control list? (Choose two.)
  A. ACLs provide a basic level of security for network access.
  B. ACLs can control which areas a host can access on a network.
  C. Standard ACLs can restrict access to specific applications and ports.
  D. ACLs assist the router in determining the best path to a destination.
  E. ACLs can permit or deny traffic based upon the MAC address originating on the router.

Answer: A, B.

Explanation
ACLs can be used for the following:Limit network traffic in order to provide adequate network performance Restrict the delivery of routing updates Provide a basic level of security Filter traffic based on the type of traffic being sent Filter traffic based on IP addressing

Question 71:
A client is using SLAAC to obtain an IPv6 address for the interface. After an address has been generated and applied to the interface, what must the client do before it can begin to use this IPv6 address?

69

A. It must send an ICMPv6 Router Solicitation message to determine what default gateway it should use.
B. It must send an ICMPv6 Router Solicitation message to request the address of the DNS server.
C. It must send an ICMPv6 Neighbor Solicitation message to ensure that the address is not already in use on the network.
D. It must wait for an ICMPv6 Router Advertisement message giving permission to use this address.

Answer: C.

Explanation
Stateless DHCPv6 or stateful DHCPv6 uses a DHCP server, but Stateless Address Autoconfiguration (SLAAC) does not. A SLAAC client can automatically generate an address that is based on information from local routers via Router Advertisement (RA) messages. Once an address has been assigned to an interface via SLAAC, the client must ensure via Duplicate Address Detection (DAD) that the address is not already in use. It does this by sending out an ICMPv6 Neighbor Solicitation message and listening for a response. If a response is received, then it means that another device is already using this address.

Question 72:
A technician is troubleshooting a network connectivity problem. Pings to the local wireless router are successful but pings to a server on the Internet are unsuccessful. Which CLI command could assist the technician to find the location of the networking problem?
A. tracert
B. ipconfig
C. msconfig
D. ipconfig/renew

Answer: A.

Explanation
The tracert utility (also known as the tracert command or tracert tool) will enable the technician to locate the link to the server that is down. The ipconfig command displays the computer network configuration details. The ipconfig/renew command requests an IP address from a DHCP server. Msconfig is not a network troubleshooting command.

Question 73:
What are two evasion techniques that are used by hackers? (Choose two.)
A. Trojan horse
B. pivot
C. rootkit
D. reconnaissance

E. phishing

Answer: B, C.

Explanation
The following methods are used by hackers to avoid detection:
- **Encryption and tunneling** – hide or scramble the malware content
- **Resource exhaustion** – keeps the host device too busy to detect the invasion
- **Traffic fragmentation** – splits the malware into multiple packets
- **Protocol-level misinterpretation** – sneaks by the firewall
- **Pivot** – uses a compromised network device to attempt access to another device
- **Rootkit** – allows the hacker to be undetected and hides software installed by the hacker

Question 74:
When a security attack has occurred, which two approaches should security professionals take to mitigate a compromised system during the Actions on Objectives step as defined by the Cyber Kill Chain model? (Choose two.)
   A. Perform forensic analysis of endpoints for rapid triage.
   B. Train web developers for securing code.
   C. Build detections for the behavior of known malware.
   D. Collect malware files and metadata for future analysis.
   E. Detects data exfiltration, lateral movement, and unauthorized credential usage.

Answer: A, E.

Explanation
When security professionals are alerted about the system compromises, forensic analysis of endpoints should be performed immediately for rapid triage. In addition, detection efforts for further attacking activities such as data exfiltration, lateral movement, and unauthorized credential usage should be enhanced to reduce damage to the minimum

Question 75:
Which field in the TCP header indicates the status of the three-way handshake process?
   A. control bits
   B. window
   C. reserved
   D. checksum

Answer: A.

Explanation
The value in the control bits field of theTCP header indicates the progress and status of the connection.

Question 76:
A user opens three browsers on the same PC to access www.cisco.com to search for certification course information. The Cisco web server sends a datagram as a reply to the request from one of the web browsers. Which information is used by the TCP/IP protocol stack in the PC to identify which of the three web browsers should receive the reply?
  A. the source IP address
  B. the destination port number
  C. the destination IP address
  D. the source port number

Answer: B.

Explanation
Each web browser client application opens a randomly generated port number in the range of the registered ports and uses this number as the source port number in the datagram that it sends to a server. The server then uses this port number as the destination port number in the reply datagram that it sends to the web browser. The PC that is running the web browser application receives the datagram and uses the destination port number that is contained in this datagram to identify the client application.

Question 77:
What are two scenarios where probabilistic security analysis is best suited? (Choose two.)
  A. when applications that conform to application/networking standards are analyzed
  B. when analyzing events with the assumption that they follow predefined steps
  C. when random variables create difficulty in knowing with certainty the outcome of any given event
  D. when analyzing applications designed to circumvent firewalls
  E. when each event is the inevitable result of antecedent causes

Answer: B, D.

Question 78:
Which tool is a web application that provides the cybersecurity analyst an easy-to-read means of viewing an entire Layer 4 session?
  A. Snort
  B. Zeek
  C. CapME
  D. OSSEC

Answer: C.

Question 79:

What are two characteristics of the SLAAC method for IPv6 address configuration? (Choose two.)

A. The default gateway of an IPv6 client on a LAN will be the link-local address of the router interface attached to the LAN.
B. This stateful method of acquiring an IPv6 address requires at least one DHCPv6 server.
C. Clients send router advertisement messages to routers to request IPv6 addressing.
D. IPv6 addressing is dynamically assigned to clients through the use of ICMPv6.
E. Router solicitation messages are sent by the router to offer IPv6 addressing to clients.

Answer: A.

Question 80:
A technician notices that an application is not responding to commands and that the computer seems to respond slowly when applications are opened. What is the best administrative tool to force the release of system resources from the unresponsive application?

A. Event Viewer
B. System Restore
C. Add or Remove Programs
D. Task Manager

Answer: D.

Explanation
Use the Task Manager Performance tab to see a visual representation of CPU and RAM utilization. This is helpful in determining if more memory is needed. Use the Applications tab to halt an application that is not responding.

Question 81:
How can statistical data be used to describe or predict network behavior?

A. by comparing normal network behavior to current network behavior
B. by recording conversations between network endpoints
C. by listing results of user web surfing activities
D. by displaying alert messages that are generated by Snort

Answer: A.

Explanation
Statistical data is created through the analysis of other forms of network data. Statistical characteristics of normal network behavior can be compared to current network traffic in an effort to detect anomalies. Conclusions resulting from analysis can be used to describe or predict network behavior.

Question 82:

Which metric in the CVSS Base Metric Group is used with an attack vector?
- A. the proximity of the threat actor to the vulnerability
- B. the presence or absence of the requirement for user interaction in order for an exploit to be successful
- C. the determination whether the initial authority changes to a second authority during the exploit
- D. the number of components, software, hardware, or networks, that are beyond the control of the attacker and that must be present in order for a vulnerability to be successfully exploited

Answer: A.

Explanation
This is a metric that reflects the proximity of the threat actor to the vulnerable component. The more remote the threat actor is to the component, the higher the severity. Threat actors close to your network or inside your network are easier to detect and mitigate.
The attack vector is one of several metrics defined in the Common Vulnerability Scoring System (CVSS) Base Metric Group Exploitability metrics. The attack vector is how close the threat actor is to the vulnerable component. The farther away the threat actor is to the component, the higher the severity because threat actors close to the network are easier to detect and mitigate.

Question 83:
Which NIST Cybersecurity Framework core function is concerned with the development and implementation of safeguards that ensure the delivery of critical infrastructure services?
- A. respond
- B. detect
- C. identify
- D. recover
- E. protect

Answer: E.

Question 84:
Which two techniques are used in a smurf attack? (Choose two.)
- A. session hijacking
- B. resource exhaustion
- C. botnets
- D. amplification
- E. reflection

Answer: D, E.

Question 85:

What is the primary objective of a threat intelligence platform (TIP)?
- A. to aggregate the data in one place and present it in a comprehensible and usable format
- B. to provide a specification for an application layer protocol that allows the communication of CTI over HTTPS
- C. to provide a standardized schema for specifying, capturing, characterizing, and communicating events and properties of network operations
- D. to provide a security operations platform that integrates and enhances diverse security tools and threat intelligence

Answer: D.

Question 86:
Which wireless parameter is used by an access point to broadcast frames that include the SSID?
- A. security mode
- B. active mode
- C. passive mode
- D. channel setting

Answer: C.

Explanation
The two scanning or probing modes an access point can be placed into are passive or active. In passive mode, the AP advertises the SSID, supported standards, and security settings in broadcast beacon frames. In active mode, the wireless client must be manually configured for the same wireless parameters as the AP has configured.

Question 87:
An employee connects wirelessly to the company network using a cell phone. The employee then configures the cell phone to act as a wireless access point that will allow new employees to connect to the company network. Which type of security threat best describes this situation?
- A. rogue access point
- B. cracking
- C. denial of service
- D. spoofing

Answer: A.

Explanation
Configuring the cell phone to act as a wireless access point means that the cell phone is now a rogue access point. The employee unknowingly breached the security of the company network by allowing a user to access the network without connecting through the company access point. Cracking is the process of obtaining passwords from data stored or transmitted on a network.

Denial of service attacks refer to sending large amounts of data to a networked device, such as a server, to prevent legitimate access to the server. Spoofing refers to access gained to a network or data by an attacker appearing to be a legitimate network device or user.

Question 88:
What information is required for a WHOIS query?
A. outside global address of the client
B. ICANN lookup server address
C. link-local address of the domain owner
D. FQDN of the domain

Answer: D.

Question 89:
Which two statements describe the characteristics of symmetric algorithms? (Choose two.)
A. They are referred to as a pre-shared key or secret key.
B. They use a pair of a public key and a private key.
C. They are commonly used with VPN traffic.
D. They provide confidentiality, integrity, and availability.

Answer: A, C.

Explanation
Symmetric encryption algorithms use the same key (also called shared secret) to encrypt and decrypt the data. In contrast, asymmetric encryption algorithms use a pair of keys, one for encryption and another for decryption.

Question 90:
What are two drawbacks to using HIPS? (Choose two.)
A. With HIPS, the success or failure of an attack cannot be readily determined.
B. With HIPS, the network administrator must verify support for all the different operating systems used in the network.
C. HIPS has difficulty constructing an accurate network picture or coordinating events that occur across the entire network.
D. If the network traffic stream is encrypted, HIPS is unable to access unencrypted forms of the traffic.
E. HIPS installations are vulnerable to fragmentation attacks or variable HL attacks

Answer: B, C.

Question 91:
What are the three functions provided by the syslog service? (Choose three.)
A. to select the type of logging information that is captured

B. to periodically poll agents for data
C. to provide statistics on packets that are flowing through a Cisco device
D. to provide traffic analysis
E. to gather logging information for monitoring and troubleshooting
F. to specify the destinations of captured messages

Answer: A, E, F.

Explanation
There are three primary functions provided by the syslog service: gathering logging information selection of the type of information to be logged selection of the destination of the logged information

Question 92:
Which consideration is important when implementing syslog in a network?
A. Enable the highest level of syslog available to ensure logging of all possible event messages.
B. Synchronize clocks on all network devices with a protocol such as Network Time Protocol.
C. Log all messages to the system buffer so that they can be displayed when accessing the router.
D. Use SSH to access syslog information

Answer: B.

Question 93:
What are the two ways threat actors use NTP? (Choose two.)
A. They place an attachment inside an email message.
B. They attack the NTP infrastructure in order to corrupt the information used to log the attack.
C. They place iFrames on a frequently used corporate web page.
D. They encode stolen data as the subdomain portion where the nameserver is under control of an attacker.
E. Threat actors use NTP systems to direct DDoS attacks.

Answer: B, E.

Question 94:
Which two features are included by both TACACS+ and RADIUS protocols? (Choose two.)
A. password encryption
B. separate authentication and authorization processes
C. SIP support
D. utilization of transport layer protocols

E. 802.IX support

Answer: A, D.

Explanation
Both TACACS+ and RADIUS support password encryption (TACACS+ encrypts all communlcatlon) and use Layer 4 protocol (IACACS+ uses TCP and RADIUS uses UDP). TACACS+ supports separation of authentication and authorization processes, while RADIUS combines authentication and authorization as one process. RADIUS supports remote access technology, such as 802.1x and SIP; TACACS+ does not.

Question 95:
What are two types of attacks used on DNS open resolvers? (Choose two.)
    A. amplification and reflection
    B. fast flux
    C. ARP poisoning
    D. resource utilization
    E. cushioning

Answer: A, D.

Explanation
Three types of attacks used on DNS open resolvers are as follows:
DNS cache poisoning – attacker sends spoofed falsified information to redirect users from legitimate sites to malicious sites.

DNS poisoning

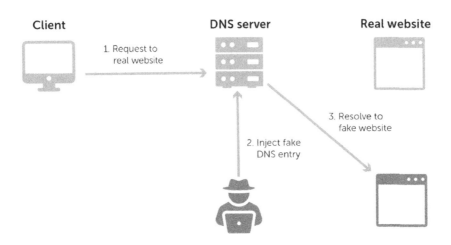

DNS amplification and reflection attacks – attacker sends an increased volume of attacks to mask the true source of the attack.

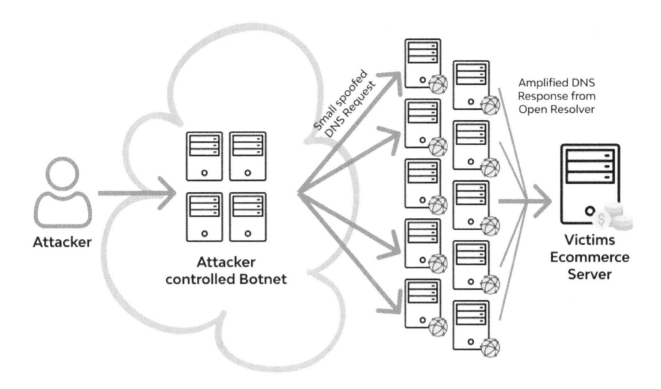

DNS resource utilization attacks – a denial of service (DoS) attack that consumes server resources.

Chapter 4: 200-201 CBROPS Mock Test #3

Question 1:
Which term is used to describe the process of identifying the NSM-related data to be gathered?
- A. data archiving
- B. data normalization
- C. data reduction
- D. data retention

Answer: C.

Question 2:
According to NIST, which step in the digital forensics process involves preparing and presenting information that resulted from scrutinizing data?
- A. examination
- B. collection
- C. reporting
- D. analysis

Answer: C.

Explanation
NIST describes the digital forensics process as involving the following four steps:

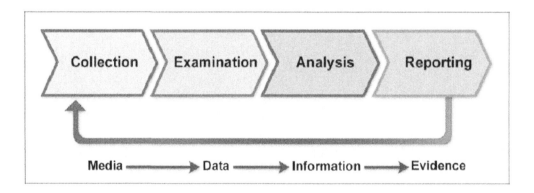

- **Collection** – the identification of potential sources of forensic data and acquisition, handling, and storage of that data
- **Examination** – assessing and extracting relevant information from the collected data. This may involve decompression or decryption of the data
- **Analysis** – drawing conclusions from the data. Salient features, such as people, places, times, events, and so on should be documented

- **Reporting** – preparing and presenting information that resulted from the analysis. Reporting should be impartial and alternative explanations should be offered if appropriate

Question 3:
Which two options are window managers for Linux? (Choose two.)

A. File Explorer
B. Kali
C. Gnome
D. PenTesting
E. KDE

Answer: C, E.

Question 4:
What are the two methods that a wireless NIC can use to discover an AP? (Choose two.)

A. transmitting a probe request
B. sending an ARP request broadcast
C. initiating a three-way handshake
D. receiving a broadcast beacon frame
E. sending a multicast frame

Answer: A, D.

Explanation
Two methods can be used by a wireless device to discover and register with an access point: passive mode and active mode. In passive mode, the AP sends a broadcast beacon frame that contains the SSID and other wireless settings. In active mode, the wireless device must be manually configured for the SSID, and then the device broadcasts a probe request.

Question 5:
A client device has initiated a secure HTTP request to a web browser. Which well-known port address number is associated with the destination address?

A. 110
B. 80
C. 443
D. 404

Answer: C.

Explanation
Port numbers are used in TCP and UDP communications to differentiate between the various services running on a device. The well-known port number used by HTTPs is port 443.

Question 6:
Which term describes evidence that is in its original state?
  A. Corroborating evidence
  B. Best evidence
  C. Indirect evidence
  D. Direct evidence

Answer: B.

Explanation
Evidence can be classified as follows:
  • **Best evidence:** This is evidence that is in its original state. It might be storage devices used by an accused or archives of files that can be proven to be unaltered.
  • **Corroborating evidence:** This is evidence that supports a proposition already supported by initial evidence, therefore confirming the original proposition.
  • **Indirect evidence:** This evidence acts in combination with other facts to establish a hypothesis.

Question 7:
Which three statements describe a DHCP Discover message? (Choose three.)
  A. The source MAC address is 48 ones (FF-FF-FF-FF-FF-FF).
  B. The destination IP address is 255.255.255.255.
  C. The message comes from a server offering an IP address.
  D. The message comes from a client seeking an IP address.
  E. All hosts receive the message, but only a DHCP server replies.
  F. Only the DHCP server receives the message.

Answer: B, D, E.

Explanation
When a host configured to use DHCP powers up on a network it sends a DHCPDISCOVER message. FF-FF-FF-FF-FF-FF is the L2 broadcast address. A DHCP server replies with a unicast DHCPOFFER message back to the host.

Question 8:
Which step in the Vulnerability Management Life Cycle categorizes assets into groups or business units, and assigns a business value to asset groups based on their criticality to business operations?
  A. remediate
  B. prioritize assets
  C. report
  D. assess

Answer: B.

Question 9:

What are two motivating factors for nation-state sponsored threat actors? (Choose two.)
- A. industrial espionage
- B. showing off their hacking skill
- C. disruption of trade or infrastructure
- D. social or personal causes
- E. financial gain

Answer: A, C.

Explanation

Nation-state threat actors are not typically interested or motivated by financial gain. They are primarily involved in corporate espionage or disrupting international trade or critical infrastructure.

Question 10:

Which type of data is used by Cisco Cognitive Intelligence to find malicious activity that has bypassed security controls, or entered through unmonitored channels, and is operating inside an enterprise network?
- A. statistical
- B. session
- C. alert
- D. transaction

Answer: A.

Explanation

Cisco Cognitive Intelligence utilizes statistical data for statistical analysis in order to find malicious activity that has bypassed security controls, or entered through unmonitored channels (including removable media), and is operating inside the network of an organization.

Question 11:

Which type of evasion technique splits malicious payloads into smaller packets in order to bypass security sensors that do not reassemble the payloads before scanning them?
- A. pivoting
- B. traffic fragmentation
- C. protocol-level misinterpretation
- D. traffic insertion

Answer: B.

Explanation

In order to keep the malicious payload from being recognized by security sensors, such as IPS or IDS, perpetrators fragment the data into smaller packets.These fragments can be passed by sensors that do not reassemble the data before scanning.

Question 12:

Which type of cyber attack is a form of MiTM in which the perpetrator copies IP packets off the network without modifying them?
    A. compromised key
    B. eavesdropping
    C. denial-of-service
    D. IP spoofing

Answer: B.

Explanation
An eavesdropping attack is a form of man-in-the-middle in which the perpetrator just reads or copies IP packets off the network but does not alter them.

Question 13:

Which is an example of social engineering?
    A. an anonymous programmer directing a DDoS attack on a data center
    B. an unidentified person claiming to be a technician collecting user information from employees
    C. a computer displaying unauthorized pop-ups and adware
    D. the infection of a computer by a virus carried by a Trojan

Answer: B.

Explanation
A social engineer attempts to gain the confidence of an employee and convince that person to divulge confidential and sensitive information, such as usernames and passwords. DDoS attacks, pop-ups, and viruses are all examples of software based security threats, not social engineering.

Question 14:

Which component is a pillar of the zero trust security approach that focuses on the secure access of devices, such as servers, printers, and other endpoints, including devices attached to IoT?
    A. workflows
    B. workloads
    C. workplace
    D. workforce

Answer: C.

Explanation
The workplace pillar focuses on secure access for any and all devices, including devices on the internet of things (IoT), which connect to enterprise networks, such as user endpoints, physical and virtual servers, printers, cameras, HVAC systems, kiosks, infusion pumps, industrial control systems, and more.

Question 15:
A security analyst is reviewing information contained in a Wireshark capture created during an attempted intrusion. The analyst wants to correlate the Wireshark information with the log files from two servers that may have been compromised. What type of information can be used to correlate the events found in these multiple data sets?
   A. ISP geolocation data
   B. IP five-tuples
   C. logged-in user account
   D. ownership metadata

Answer: B.

Explanation
The source and destination IP address, ports, and protocol (the IP five-tuples) can be used to correlate different data sets when analyzing an intrusion.

Question 16:
A security analyst is investigating a cyber attack that began by compromising one file system through a vulnerability in a custom software application. The attack now appears to be affecting additional file systems under the control of another security authority. Which CVSS v3.0 base exploitability metric score is increased by this attack characteristic?
   A. privileges required
   B. scope
   C. attack complexity
   D. user interaction

Answer: B.

Explanation
The scope metric is impacted by an exploited vulnerability that can affect resources beyond the authorized privileges of the vulnerable component or that are managed by a different security authority.

Question 17:
Which regular expression would match any string that contains 4 consecutive zeros?
   A. {0-4}

B. [0-4]
C. 0{4}
D. ^0000

Answer: C.

Explanation
The regular expression 0{4} matches any string that contains 4 repetitions of zero or 4 consecutive zeros.

Question 18:
Using Tcpdump and Wireshark, a security analyst extracts a downloaded file from a pcap file. The analyst suspects that the file is a virus and wants to know the file type for further examination. Which Linux command can be used to determine the file type?
    A. file
    B. tail
    C. nano
    D. ls -l

Answer: A.

Explanation
The Linux file command can be used to determine a file type, such as whether it is executable, ASCII text, or zip.

Question 19:
Which one of the following is an advantage of an IPS?
    A. It can stop malicious packets.
    B. It is deployed in offline mode.
    C. It has no impact on latency.
    D. It is primarily focused on identifying possible incidents.

Answer: A.

Explanation
An advantage of intrusion prevention systems (IPS) is that it can identify and stop malicious packets. However, because an IPS is deployed inline, it can add latency to the network.

Question 20:
Which three fields are found in both the TCP and UDP headers? (Choose three.)
    A. window
    B. checksum
    C. options
    D. sequence number

E. destination port
F. source port

Answer: B, E, F.

Explanation
The UPD header has four fields. Three of these fields are in common with the TCP header. These three fields are the source port, destination port, and checksum.

Question 21:
What will match the regular expression ^83?
A. any string that includes 83
B. any string that begins with 83
C. any string with values greater than 83
D. any string that ends with 83

Answer: B.

Explanation
The expression ^83 indicates any string that begins with 83 will be matched.

Question 22:
Which two actions can be taken when configuring Windows Firewall? (Choose two.)
A. Turn on port screening.
B. Manually open ports that are required for specific applications.
C. Allow a different software firewall to control access.
D. Enable MAC address authentication.
E. Perform a rollback.

Answer: B, C.

Explanation
When a different software firewall is installed, Windows Firewall must be disabled through the Windows Firewall control panel. When Windows Firewall is enabled, specific ports can be enabled that are needed by specific applications.

Question 23:
What is one difference between the client-server and peer-to-peer network models?
A. Only in the client-server model can file transfers occur.
B. A data transfer that uses a device serving in a client role requires that a dedicated server be present.
C. A peer-to-peer network transfers data faster than a transfer using a client server network.
D. Every device in a peer-to-peer network can function as a client or a server.

Answer: D.

Question 24:
What classification is used for an alert that correctly identifies that an exploit has occurred?
    A. false negatlve
    B. false positive
    C. true positive
    D. true negative

Answer: C.

Explanation
A true positive occurs when an IDS and IPS signature is correctly fired and an alarm is generated when offending traffic is detected.

Question 25:
During the detection and analysis phase of the NIST incident response process life cycle, which sign category is used to describe that an incident might occur in the future?
    A. attrition
    B. impersonation
    C. precursor
    D. indicator

Answer: C.

Explanation
There are two categories for the signs of an incident:
- **Precursor** – a sign that an incident might occur in the future.
- **Indicator** – a sign that an incident might already have occurred or is currently occurring.

Question 26:
According to the Cyber Kill Chain model, after a weapon is delivered to a targeted system, what is the next step that a threat actor would take?
    A. action on objectives
    B. exploitation
    C. weaponization
    D. installation

Answer: B.

Explanation

The Cyber Kill Chain specifies seven steps (or phases) and sequences that a threat actor must complete to accomplish an attack:

- **Reconnaissance** – The threat actor performs research, gathers intelligence, and selects targets.
- **Weaponization** – The threat actor uses the information from the reconnaissance phase to develop a weapon against specific targeted systems.
- **Delivery** – The weapon is transmitted to the target using a delivery vector.
- **Exploitation** – The threat actor uses the weapon delivered to break the vulnerability and gain control of the target.
- **Installation** – The threat actor establishes a backdoor into the system to allow for continued access to the target.
- **Command and Control (CnC)** – The threat actor establishes command and control (CnC) with the target system.
- **Action on Objectives** – The threat actor is able to take action on the target system, thus achieving the original objective.

Our considered steps for Ransomware feature taxonomy

Cyber Kill Chain (CKC) seven steps

Question 27:
A company is applying the NIST.SP800-61 r2 incident handling process to security events. What are two examples of incidents that are in the category of precursor? (Choose two.)
A. multiple failed logins from an unknown source
B. log entries that show a response to a port scan
C. an IDS alert message being sent
D. a newly-discovered vulnerability in Apache web servers
E. a host that has been verified as infected with malware

Answer: B, D.

Explanation

89

As an incident category, the precursor is a sign that an incident might occur in the future. Examples of precursors are log entries that show a response to a port scan or a newly-discovered vulnerability in web servers using Apache.

Question 28:
Which regulatory law regulates the identification, storage, and transmission of patient personal healthcare information?
   A. FISMA
   B. HIPAA
   C. PCI-DSS
   D. GLBA

Answer: B.

Explanation
The Health Insurance Portability and Accountability Act (HIPAA) requires that all patient personally identifiable healthcare information be stored, maintained, and transmitted in ways that ensure patient privacy and confidentiality.

Question 29:
Which NIST-defined incident response stakeholder is responsible for coordinating incident response with other stakeholders and minimizing the damage of an incident?
   A. human resources
   B. IT support
   C. the legal department
   D. management

Answer: D.

Explanation
The management team creates the policies, designs the budget, and is in charge of staffing all departments. Management is also responsible for coordinating the incident response with other stakeholders and minimizing the damage of an incident.

Question 30:
What is defined in the policy element of the NIST incident response plan?
   A. how to handle incidents based on the mission and functions of an organization
   B. a roadmap for updating the incident response capability
   C. the metrics used for measuring incident response capability in an organization
   D. how the incident response team of an organization will communicate with organization stakeholders

Answer: A.

Explanation
The policy element of the NIST incident response plan details how incidents should be handled based on the mission and function of the organization.

Question 31:
What is the responsibility of the human resources department when handling a security incident as defined by NIST?
   A. Review the incident policies, plans, and procedures for local or federal guideline violations.
   B. Perform disciplinary actions if an incident is caused by an employee.
   C. Coordinate the incident response with other stakeholders and minimize the damage of an incident.
   D. Perform actions to minimize the effectiveness of the attack and preserve evidence.

Answer: B.

Explanation
The human resources department may be called upon to perform disciplinary measures if an incident is caused by an employee.

Question 32:
What is the benefit of a defense-in-depth approach?
   A. All network vulnerabilities are mitigated.
   B. The need for firewalls is eliminated.
   C. Only a single layer of security at the network core is required.
   D. The effectiveness of other security measures is not impacted when a security mechanism fails.

Answer: D.

Explanation
The benefit of the defense-in-depth approach is that network defenses are implemented in layers so that failure of any single security mechanism does not impact other security measures.

Question 33:
Which type of analysis relies on predefined conditions and can analyze applications that only use well-known fixed ports?
   A. statistical
   B. deterministic
   C. log
   D. probabilistic

Answer: B.

Explanation
Deterministic analysis uses predefined conditions to analyze applications that conform to specification standards, such as performing a port-based analysis.

Question 34:
Which type of analysis relies on different methods to establish the likelihood that a security event has happened or will happen?
    A. deterministic
    B. statistical
    C. log
    D. probabilistic

Answer: D.

Explanation
Probabilistic methods use powerful tools to create a probabilistic answer as a result of analyzing applications.

Question 35:
Which access control model allows users to control access to data as an owner of that data?
    A. mandatory access control
    B. non discretionary access control
    C. discretionary access control
    D. attribute-based access control

Answer: C.

Explanation
In the discretionary access control (DAC) model, users can control access to data as owners of the data.

Question 36:
A user calls the help desk complaining that the password to access the wireless network has changed without warning. The user is allowed to change the password, but an hour later, the same thing occurs. What might be happening in this situation?
    A. rogue access point
    B. password policy
    C. weak password
    D. user error
    E. user laptop

Answer: A.

Explanation
Man-in-the-middle attacks are a threat that results in lost credentials and data. These types of attacks can occur for different reasons including traffic sniffing.

Question 37:
Which access control model applies the strictest access control and is often used in military and mission critical applications?
  A. discretionary
  B. mandatory
  C. nondiscretionary
  D. attribute-based

Answer: B.

Explanation
Military and mission critical applications typically use mandatory access control which applies the strictest access control to protect network resources.

Question 38:
What is the principle behind the non discretionary access control model?
  A. It applies the strictest access control possible.
  B. It allows access decisions to be based on roles and responsibilities of a user within the organization.
  C. It allows users to control access to their data as owners of that data.
  D. It allows access based on attributes of the object to be accessed.

Answer: B.

Explanation
The non discretionary access control model used the roles and responsibilities of the user as the basis for access decisions.

Question 39:
Which attack is integrated with the lowest levels of the operating system of a host and attempts to completely hide the activities of the threat actor on the local system?
  A. rootkit
  B. traffic insertion
  C. traffic substitution
  D. encryption and tunneling

Answer: A.

Explanation

A rootkit is a complex attack tool and it integrates with the lowest levels of the operating system. The goal of the rootkit is to completely hide the activities of the threat actor on the local system.

Question 40:

A company has just had a cybersecurity incident. The threat actor appeared to have a goal of network disruption and appeared to use a common security hack tool that overwhelmed a particular server with a large amount of traffic. This traffic rendered the server inoperable. How would a certified cybersecurity analyst classify this type of threat actor?
   A. terrorist
   B. hacktivist
   C. state-sponsored
   D. amateur

Answer: D.

Explanation
Amateurs or script kiddies use common, existing tools found on the internet to launch attacks. Hacktivists disrupt services in protest against organizations or governments for a particular political or social idea. State-sponsored threat actors use cyberspace for industrial espionage or interfering with another country in some way.

Question 41:

To which category of security attacks does man-in-the-middle belong?
   A. DoS
   B. access
   C. reconnaissance
   D. social engineering

Answer: B.

Explanation
With a man-in-the-middle attack, a threat actor is positioned in between two legitimate entities in order to read, modify, or redirect the data that passes between the two parties.

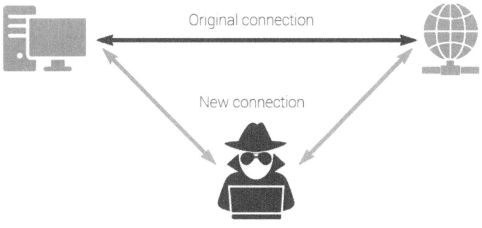

Original connection

New connection

Man in the middle, Phisher,
or annonymous proxy

Question 42:
What is an example of a local exploit?
- A. Port scanning is used to determine if the Telnet service is running on a remote server.
- B. A threat actor performs a brute force attack on an enterprise edge router to gain illegal access.
- C. A buffer overflow attack is launched against an online shopping website and causes the server crash.
- D. A threat actor tries to gain the user password of a remote host by using a keyboard capture software installed on it by a Trojan.

Answer: D.

Explanation
Vulnerability exploits may be remote or local. In a local exploit, the threat actor has some type of user access to the end system, either physically or through remote access. The exploitation activity is within the local network.

Question 43:
Which Cisco appliance can be used to filter network traffic contents to report and deny traffic based on the web server reputation?
- A. WSA
- B. AVC
- C. ASA
- D. ESA

Answer: A.

Explanation
The Cisco Web Security Appliance (WSA) acts as a web proxy for an enterprise network. WSA can provide many types of logs related to web traffic security including ACL decision logs, malware scan logs, and web reputation filtering logs. The Cisco Email Security Appliance (ESA) is a tool to monitor most aspects of email delivery, system functioning, antivirus, antispam operations, and blacklist and whitelist decisions. The Cisco ASA is a firewall appliance. The Cisco Application Visibility and Control (AVC) system combines multiple technologies to recognize, analyze, and control over 1000 applications

Question 44:
Which evasion method describes the situation that after gaining access to the administrator password on a compromised host, a threat actor is attempting to login to another host using the same credentials?
- A. pivoting
- B. traffic substitution
- C. resource exhaustion
- D. protocol-level misinterpretation

Answer: A.

Explanation
Pivoting is an evasion method that assumes the threat actor has compromised an inside host and the actor wants to expand the access further into the compromised network.

Question 45:
What are two examples of DoS attacks? (Choose two.)
- A. port scanning
- B. SQL injection
- C. ping of death
- D. phishing
- E. buffer overflow

Answer: C, E.

Explanation
The buffer overflow and ping of death DoS attacks exploit system memory-related flaws on a server by sending an unexpected amount of data or malformed data to the server.

Question 46:
Which type of attack is carried out by threat actors against a network to determine which IP addresses, protocols, and ports are allowed by ACLs?
- A. social engineering
- B. denial of service

C. phishing

D. reconnaissance

Answer: D.

Explanation

Packet filtering ACLs use rules to filter incoming and outgoing traffic. These rules are defined by specifying IP addresses, port numbers, and protocols to be matched. Threat actors can use a reconnaissance attack involving port scanning or penetration testing to determine which IP addresses, protocols, and ports are allowed by ACLs.

Question 47:

Which two attacks target web servers through exploiting possible vulnerabilities of input functions used by an application? (Choose two.)

A. SQL injection

B. port scanning

C. port redirection

D. trust exploitation

E. cross-site scripting

Answer: A, E.

Explanation

When a web application uses input fields to collect data from clients, threat actors may exploit possible vulnerabilities for entering malicious commands. The malicious commands that are executed through the web application might affect the OS on the web server. SQL injection and cross-site scripting are two different types of command injection attacks.

Question 48:

Which security function is provided by encryption algorithms?

A. key management

B. authorization

C. integrity

D. confidentiality

Answer: D.

Explanation

Encryption algorithms are used to provide data confidentiality, which ensures that if data is intercepted in transit, it cannot be read.

Question 49:

Which security endpoint setting would be used by a security analyst to determine if a computer has been configured to prevent a particular application from running?

A. baselining
B. blacklisting
C. services
D. whitelisting

Answer: B.

Explanation
Blacklisting can be used on a local system or updated on security devices such as a firewall. Blacklists can be manually entered or obtained from a centralized security system. Blacklists are applications that are prevented from executing because they pose a security risk to the individual system and potentially the company.

Question 50:
At the request of investors, a company is proceeding with cyber attribution with a particular attack that was conducted from an external source. Which security term is used to describe the person or device responsible for the attack?
A. threat actor
B. fragmenter
C. tunneler
D. skeleton

Answer: A.

Explanation
Some people may use the common word of "hacker" to describe a threat actor. A threat actor is an entity that is involved with an incident that impacts or has the potential to impact an organization in such a way that it is considered a security risk or threat.

Question 51:
Which Windows application is commonly used by a cybersecurity analyst to view Microsoft IIS access logs?
A. Event Viewer
B. Notepad
C. SIEM
D. Word

Answer: A.

Explanation
Event Viewer is an application on a Windows-based device used to view event logs including IIS access logs.

Question 52:

Which two algorithms use a hashing function to ensure message integrity? (Choose two.)

A. SEAL

B. AES

C. 3DES

D. MD5

E. SHA

Answer: D, E.

Explanation

Indirect evidence cannot prove a fact on its own, but direct evidence can. Corroborative evidence is supporting information. Best evidence is most reliable because it is something concrete such as a signed contract.

Question 53:

After complaints from users, a technician identifies that the college web server is running very slowly. A check of the server reveals that there are an unusually large number of TCP requests coming from multiple locations on the Internet. What is the source of the problem?

A. The server is infected with a virus.

B. A DDoS attack is in progress.

C. There is insufficient bandwidth to connect to the server.

D. There is a replay attack in progress.

Answer: B.

Explanation

The source of the problem cannot be a virus because in this situation the server is passive and at the receiving end of the attack. A replay attack uses intercepted and recorded data in an attempt to gain access to an unauthorized server. This type of attack does not involve multiple computers. The issue is not the bandwidth available, but the number of TCP connections taking place. Receiving a large number of connections from multiple locations is the main symptom of a distributed denial of service attack which uses botnets or zombie computers.

Question 54:

Which statement describes a typical security policy for a DMZ firewall configuration?

A. Traffic that originates from the DMZ interface is selectively permitted to the outside interface.

B. Return traffic from the inside that is associated with traffic originating from the outside is permitted to traverse from the inside interface to the outside interface.

C. Return traffic from the outside that is associated with traffic originating from the inside is permitted to traverse from the outside interface to the DMZ interface.

D. Traffic that originates from the inside interface is generally blocked entirely or very selectively permitted to the outside interface.

E. Traffic that originates from the outside interface is permitted to traverse the firewall to the inside interface with few or no restrictions.

Answer: A.

Explanation

With a three interface firewall design that has internal, external, and DMZ connections, typical configurations include the following: Traffic originating from DMZ destined for the internal network is normally blocked. Traffic originating from the DMZ destined for external networks is typically permitted based on what services are being used in the DMZ. Traffic originating from the internal network destined from the DMZ is normally inspected and allowed to return. Traffic originating from external networks (the public network) is typically allowed in the DMZ only for specific services.

Question 55:

What are two shared characteristics of the IDS and the IPS? (Choose two.)

   A. Both have minimal impact on network performance.
   B. Both are deployed as sensors.
   C. Both analyze copies of network traffic.
   D. Both use signatures to detect malicious traffic.
   E. Both rely on an additional network device to respond to malicious traffic.

Answer: B, D.

Explanation

Both the IDS and the IPS are deployed as sensors and use signatures to detect malicious traffic. The IDS analyzes copies of network traffic, which results in minimal impact on network performance. The IDS also relies on an IPS to stop malicious traffic.

Question 56:

When attempting to improve system performance for Linux computers with a limited amount of memory, why is increasing the size of the swap file system not considered the best solution?

   A. A swap file system uses hard disk space to store inactive RAM content.
   B. A swap file system cannot be mounted on an MBR partition.
   C. A swap file system only supports the ex2 file system.
   D. A swap file system does not have a specific file system.

Answer: A.

Explanation

The swap file system is used by Linux when it runs out of physical memory. When needed, the kernel moves inactive RAM content to the swap partition on the hard disk. Storing and retrieving content in the swap partition is much slower than RAM is, and therefore using the swap partition should not be considered the best solution to improving system performance

Question 57:

A security professional is making recommendations to a company for enhancing endpoint security. Which security endpoint technology would be recommended as an agent-based system to protect hosts against malware?

    A. IPS
    B. HIDS
    C. baselining
    D. blacklisting

Answer: B.

Explanation
A host-based intrusion detection system (HIDS) is a comprehensive security application that provides anti-malware applications, a firewall, and monitoring and reporting.

Question 58:

Which technique could be used by security personnel to analyze a suspicious file in a safe environment?

    A. whitelisting
    B. baselining
    C. sandboxing
    D. blacklisting

Answer: C.

Explanation
Sandboxing allows suspicious files to be executed and analyzed in a safe environment. There are free public sandboxes that allow for malware samples to be uploaded or submitted and analyzed.

Question 59:

A cybersecurity analyst has been called to a crime scene that contains several technology items including a computer. Which technique will be used so that the information found on the computer can be used in court?

    A. rootkit
    B. log collection
    C. Tor
    D. unaltered disk image

Answer: D.

Explanation
A normal file copy does not recover all data on a storage device so an unaltered disk image is commonly made. An unaltered disk image preserves the original evidence, thus preventing inadvertent alteration during the discovery phase. It also allows recreation of the original evidence.

Question 60:
Which SOC technology automates security responses by using predefined playbooks which require a minimum amount of human intervention?
    A. SOAR
    B. Wireshark
    C. NetFlow
    D. SIEM
    E. syslog

Answer: A.

Explanation
SOAR technology goes a step further than SIEM by integrating threat intelligence and automating incident investigation and response workflows based on playbooks developed by the security team.

Question 61:
What is the first line of defense when an organization is using a defense-in-depth approach to network security?
    A. proxy server
    B. firewall
    C. IPS
    D. edge router

Answer: D.

Explanation
A defense-in-depth approach uses layers of security measures starting at the network edge, working through the network, and finally ending at the network endpoints. Routers at the network edge are the first line of defense and forward traffic intended for the internal network to the firewall.

Question 62:
Which access control model assigns security privileges based on the position, responsibilities, or job classification of an individual or group within an organization?
    A. rule-based

B.   role-based
C.   discretionary
D.   mandatory

Answer: B.

Explanation
Role-based access control models assign privileges based on position, responsibilities, or job classification. Users and groups with the same responsibilities or job classification share the same assigned privileges. This type of access control is also referred to as non discretionary access control.

Question 63:
Which protocol or service uses UDP for a client-to-server communication and TCP for server-to-server communication?
A.   HTTP
B.   FTP
C.   DNS
D.   SMTP

Answer: C.

Explanation
Some applications may use both TCP and UDP. DNS uses UDP when clients send requests to a DNS server, and TCP when two DNS servers directly communicate.

Question 64:
Which field in the IPv6 header points to optional network layer information that is carried in the IPv6 packet?
A.   traffic class
B.   flow label
C.   next header
D.   version

Answer: C.

Explanation
Optional Layer 3 information about fragmentation, security, and mobility is carried inside of extension headers in an IPv6 packet. The next header field of the IPv6 header acts as a pointer to these optional extension headers if they are present.

Question 65:
Which data security component is provided by hashing algorithms?
A.   integrity

B. confidentiality
C. key exchange
D. authentication

Answer: A.

Explanation
Hashing algorithms are used to provide message integrity, which ensures that data in transit has not changed or been altered.

Question 66:
Which attack surface, defined by the SANS Institute, is delivered through the exploitation of vulnerabilities in web, cloud, or host-based applications?
A. human
B. network
C. host
D. software

Answer: D.

Explanation
The SANS Institute describes three components of the attack surface:
- **Network Attack Surface** – exploits vulnerabilities in networks.
- **Software Attack Surface** – delivered through the exploitation of vulnerabilities in web, cloud, or host-based software applications.
- **Human Attack Surface** – exploits weaknesses in user behavior.

Question 67:
What is the main goal of using different evasion techniques by threat actors?
A. to launch DDoS attacks on targets
B. to identify vulnerabilities of target systems
C. to prevent detection by network and host defenses
D. to gain the trust of a corporate employee in an effort lo obtain credentials

Answer: C.

Explanation
Many threat actors use stealthy evasion techniques to disguise an attack payload because the malware and attack methods are most effective if they are undetected. The goal is to prevent detection by network and host defenses.

Question 68:
How can NAT/PAT complicate network security monitoring if NetFlow is being used?
A. It disguises the application initiated by a user by manipulating port numbers.

B. It changes the source and destination MAC addresses.

C. It conceals the contents of a packet by encrypting the data payload.

D. It hides internal IP addresses by allowing them to share one or a few outside IP addresses.

Answer: D.

Explanation

NAT/PAT maps multiple internal IP addresses with only a single or a few outside IP addresses breaking end-to-end flows. The result makes it difficult to log the inside device that is requesting and receiving the traffic. This is especially a problem with a NetFlow application because NetFlow flows are unidirectional and are defined by the addresses and ports that they share.

Question 69:

Which statement describes the function provided by the Tor network?

A. It conceals packet contents by establishing end-to-end tunnels.

B. It distributes user packets through load balancing.

C. It allows users to browse the Internet anonymously.

D. It manipulates packets by mapping IP addresses between two networks.

Answer: C.

Explanation

Tor is a software platform and network of P2P hosts that function as Internet routers on the Tor network. The Tor network allows users to browse the Internet anonymously.

Question 70:

When establishing a server profile for an organization, which element describes the type of service that an application is allowed to run on the server?

A. user account

B. listening port

C. service account

D. software environment

Answer: C.

Explanation

A server profile should contain some important elements including these:

- **Listening ports** – the TCP and UDP daemons and ports that are allowed to be open on the server
- **User accounts** – the parameters defining user access and behavior
- **Service accounts** – the definitions of the type of service that an application is allowed to run on a server

- **Software environment** – the tasks, processes, and applications that are permitted to run on the server

Question 71:
What are the three goals of a port scan attack? (Choose three.)
- A. to identify peripheral configurations
- B. to determine potential vulnerabilities
- C. to disable used ports and services
- D. to identify operating systems
- E. to identify active services
- F. to discover system passwords

Answer: B, D, E.

Question 72:
Which three things will a threat actor do to prepare a DDoS attack against a target system on the Internet? (Choose three.)
- A. Install a black door on the target system.
- B. Obtain an automated tool to deliver the malware payload.
- C. Establish two-way communications channels to the CnC infrastructure with zombies.
- D. Collect and exfiltrate data.
- E. Compromise many hosts on the Internet.
- F. Install attack software on zombies.

Answer: C, E, F.

Explanation
To prepare for launching a DDoS attack, a threat actor will compromise many hosts on the Internet, called zombies. The threat actor will then install attack software on zombies and establish a two-way communications channel to CnC infrastructure with zombies. The threat actor will issue the command to zombies through the CnC to launch a DDoS attack against a target system.

Question 73:
What is specified in the plan element of the NIST incident response plan?
- A. organizational structure and the definition of roles, responsibilities, and levels of authority
- B. metrics for measuring the incident response capability and effectiveness
- C. priority and severity ratings of incidents
- D. incident handling based on the mission of the organization

Answer: B.

Explanation

NIST recommends creating policies, plans, and procedures for establishing and maintaining a CSIRC. One component of the plan element is to develop metrics for measuring the incident response capability and its effectiveness.

Question 74:
What is the responsibility of the IT support group when handling an incident as defined by NIST?
    A. coordinates the incident response with other stakeholders and minimizes the damage of an incident
    B. performs disciplinary measures if an incident is caused by an employee
    C. performs actions to minimize the effectiveness of the attack and preserve evidence
    D. reviews the incident policies, plans, and procedures for local or federal guideline violations

Answer: C.

Explanation
IT support best understands the technology used in the organization and can perform the correct actions to minimize the effectiveness of the attack and preserve evidence.

Question 75:
What is an example of privilege escalation attack?
    A. A DDoS attack is launched against a government server and causes the server to crash.
    B. A port scanning attack finds that the FTP service is running on a server that allows anonymous access.
    C. A threat actor performs an access attack and gains the administrator password.
    D. A threat actor sends an email to an IT manager to request root access.

Answer: C.

Explanation
With the privilege escalation exploit, vulnerabilities in servers or access control systems are exploited to grant an unauthorized user, or software process, higher levels of privilege than either should have. After the higher privilege is granted, the threat actor can access sensitive information or take control of a system

Question 76:
A threat hunter is concerned about a significant increase in TCP traffic sourced from port 53. It is suspected that malicious file transfer traffic is being tunneled out using the TCP DNS port. Which deep packet inspection tool can detect the type of application originating the suspicious traffic?
    A. syslog analyzer
    B. NBAR2
    C. NetFlow

D. IDS/IPS
E. Wireshark

Answer: B.

Explanation
NBAR2 is used to discover the applications that are responsible for network traffic. NBAR is a classification engine that can recognize a wide variety of applications, including web-based applications and client/server applications.

Question 77:
Which type of evaluation includes the assessment of the likelihood of an attack, the type of threat actor likely to perpetrate such an attack, and what the consequences could be to the organization if the exploit is successful?
   A. penetration testing
   B. risk analysis
   C. vulnerability identification
   D. server profiling

Answer: B.

Question 78:
What is the dark web?
   A. It is a website that reports the most recent activities of cybercriminals all over the world.
   B. It is a website that sells stolen credit cards.
   C. It is part of the internet where a person can obtain personally identifiable information from anyone for free
   D. It is part of the internet that can only be accessed with special software.

Answer: D.

Explanation
One of the more lucrative goals of cybercriminals is obtaining lists of personally identifiable information that can then be sold on the dark web. The dark web can only be accessed with special software and is used by cybercriminals to shield their activities. Stolen PII can be used to create fake accounts, such as credit cards and short-term loans.

Question 79:
Which term describes a threat actor who has advanced skills and pursues a social agenda?
   A. organized crime
   B. script kiddie
   C. corporate/industrial spies
   D. hacktivist

Answer: D.

Question 80:
The SOC manager is reviewing the metrics for the previous calendar quarter and discovers that the MTTD for a breach of password security perpetrated through the Internet was forty days. What does the MTTD metric represent within the SOC?
   A. window of time required to stop the spread of malware in the network
   B. the average time that it takes to identify valid security incidents that have occurred
   C. the time required to stop the incident from causing further damage to systems or data
   D. the average time that it takes to stop and remediate a security incident

Answer: B.

Explanation
Cisco defines MTTD as the average time that it takes for the SOC personnel to identify that valid security incidents have occurred in the network.

Question 81:
A cybersecurity analyst is performing a CVSS assessment on an attack where a web link was sent to several employees. Once clicked, an internal attack was launched. Which CVSS Base Metric Group Exploitability metric is used to document that the user had to click on the link in order for the attack to occur?
   A. scope
   B. integrity requirement
   C. availability requirement
   D. user interaction

Answer: D.

Explanation
The CVSS Base Metric Group has the following metrics: attack vector, attack complexity, privileges required, user interaction, and scope. The user interaction metric expresses the presence or absence of the requirement for user interaction in order for an exploit to be successful.

Question 82:
When a server profile for an organization is being established, which element describes the TCP and UDP daemons and ports that are allowed to be open on the server?
   A. critical asset address space
   B. service accounts
   C. software environment
   D. listening ports

Answer: D.

Explanation
A server profile will often contain the following:
- **Listening ports** – the TCP and UDP daemons and ports that are allowed to be open on the server
- **User accounts** – the parameters defining user access and behavior
- **Service accounts** – the definitions of the type of service that an application is allowed to run on a server
- **Software environment** – the tasks, processes, and applications that are permitted to run on the server

Question 83:
Which two actions should be taken during the preparation phase of the incident response life cycle defined by NIST? (Choose two.)
   A. Fully analyze the incident.
   B. Meet with all involved parties to discuss the incident that took place.
   C. Detect all the incidents that occurred.
   D. Acquire and deploy the tools that are needed to investigate incidents.
   E. Create and train the CSIRT

Answer: D, E.

Explanation
According to the guideline defined in the NIST Incident Response Life Cycle, several actions should be taken during the preparation phase including:
- (1) creating and training the CSIRT and
- (2) acquiring and deploying the tools needed by the team to investigate incidents.

Cyber Incident Response Cycle

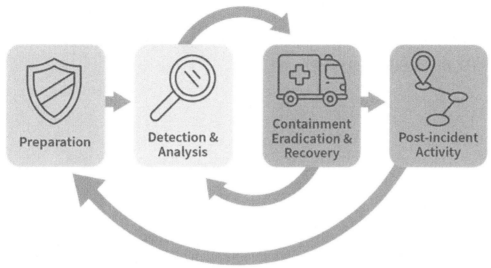

Question 84:
Which organization is an international nonprofit organization that offers the CISSP certification?
   A. CompTIA
   B. (ISC)2
   C. IEEE
   D. GIAC

Answer: B.

Explanation
(ISC)2 is an international nonprofit organization that offers the CISSP certification.

Question 85:
What is a benefit to an organization of using SOAR as part of the SIEM system?
   A. SOAR was designed to address critical security events and high-end investigation.
   B. SOAR would benefit smaller organizations because it requires no cybersecurity analyst involvement once installed.
   C. SOAR automates incident investigation and responds to workflows based on playbooks.
   D. SOAR automation guarantees an uptime factor of "5 nines'

Answer: C.

Explanation
SIEM systems are used for collecting and filtering data, detecting and classifying threats, and analyzing and investigating threats. SOAR technology does the same as SIEMs but it also includes automation. SOAR integrates threat intelligence and automates incident investigation.

SOAR also responds to events using response workflows based on previously developed playbooks.

Question 86:
Which personnel in a SOC are assigned the task of hunting for potential threats and implementing threat detection tools?
   A. Tier 3 SME
   B. Tier 2 Incident Reporter
   C. Tier 1 Analyst
   D. SOC Manager

Answer: A.

Explanation
In a SOC, Tier 3 SMEs have expert-level skills in network, endpoint, threat intelligence, and malware reverse engineering (RE). They are deeply involved in hunting for potential security threats and implementing threat detection tools.

Question 87:
What are two examples of personally identifiable information (PII)? (Choose two.)
   A. first name
   B. IP address
   C. language preference
   D. street address
   E. credit card number

Answer: D, E.

Explanation
Personally identifiable information (PII) is any data that could potentially identify and track a specific individual. A credit card number and street address are the best examples of PII.

Question 88:
The term cyber operations analyst refers to which group of personnel in a SOC?
   A. Tier 1 personnel
   B. Tier 3 personnel
   C. Tier 2 personnel
   D. SOC managers

Answer: A.

Explanation
In a typical SOC, the Tier 1 personnel are called alert analysts, also known as cyberoperations analysts.

Question 89:
When a user turns on the PC on Wednesday, the PC displays a message indicating that all of the user files have been locked. In order to get the files unencrypted, the user is supposed to send an email and include a specific ID in the email title. The message also includes ways to buy and submit bitcoins as payment for the file decryption. After inspecting the message, the technician suspects a security breach occurred. What type of malware could be responsible?
  A. Trojan
  B. spyware
  C. adware
  D. ransomware

Answer: D.

Explanation
Ransomware requires payment for access to the computer or files. Bitcoin is a type of digital currency that does not go through a particular bank.

Question 90:
An SOC is searching for a professional to fill a job opening. The employee must have expert-level skills in networking, endpoint, threat intelligence, and malware reverse engineering in order to search for cyber threats hidden within the network. Which job within an SOC requires a professional with those skills?
  A. Incident Responder
  B. Alert Analyst
  C. SOC Manager
  D. Threat Hunter

Answer: D.

Explanation
Tier 3 professionals called Threat Hunters must have expert-level skills in networking, endpoint, threat intelligence, and malware reverse engineering. They are experts at tracing the processes of malware to determine the impact of the malware and how it can be removed.

Question 91:
Which three are major categories of elements in a security operations center? (Choose three.)
  A. technologies
  B. Internet connection
  C. processes
  D. data center
  E. people

F. database engine

Answer: A, C, E.

Explanation
The three major categories of elements of a security operations center are people, processes, and technologies. A database engine, a data center, and an Internet connection are components in the technologies category.

Question 92:
Which KPI metric does SOAR use to measure the time required to stop the spread of malware in the network?
  A. MITR
  B. Time to Control
  C. MITC
  D. MUD

Answer: B.

Explanation
The common key performance indicator (KPI) metrics compiled by SOC managers are as follows:
  ● **Dwell Time:** the length of time that threat actors have access to a network before they are detected and the access of the threat actors stopped
  ● **Mean Time to Detect (MTTD):** the average time that it takes for the SOC personnel to identify that valid security incidents have occurred in the network
  ● **Mean Time to Respond (MTTR):** the average time that it takes to stop and remediate a security incident
  ● **Mean Time to contain (MTTC):** the time required to stop the incident from causing further damage to systems or data
  ● Time to Control the time required to stop the spread of malware in the network

Question 93:
What job would require verification that an alert represents a true security incident or a false positive?
  A. Alert Analyst
  B. Threat Hunter
  C. SOC Manager
  D. Incident Reporter

Answer: A.

Explanation

A Cybersecurity Analyst monitors security alert queues and uses a ticketing system to assign alerts to a queue for an analyst to investigate. Because the software that generates alerts can trigger false alarms, one job of the Cybersecurity Analyst would be to verify that an alert represents a true security incident.

Question 94:
Which technique is necessary to ensure a private transfer of data using a VPN?
   A. encryption
   B. virtualization
   C. scalability
   D. authorization

Answer: A.

Explanation
Confidential and secure transfers of data with VPNs require data encryption.

Chapter 5: 200-201 CBROPS Mock Test #4

Question 1:

Which type of tool allows administrators to observe and understand every detail of a network transaction?

  A. log manager
  B. malware analysis tool
  C. ticketing system
  D. packet capture software

Answer: D.

Explanation

Network packet capture software is an important tool because it makes it possible to observe and understand the details of a network transaction.

Question 2:

Why is Kali Linux a popular choice in testing the network security of an organization?

  A. It is a network scanning tool that prioritizes security risks.
  B. It is an open source Linux security distribution containing many penetration tools.
  C. It can be used to test weaknesses by using only malicious software.
  D. It can be used to intercept and log network traffic.

Answer: B.

Explanation

Kali is an open source Linux security distribution that is commonly used by IT professionals to test the security of networks.

Question 3:

What are two advantages of the NTFS file system compared with FAT32? (Choose two.)

  A. NTFS is easier to configure.
  B. NTFS supports large files.
  C. NTFS allows faster formatting of drives.
  D. NTFS allows the automatic detection of bad sectors.
  E. NTFS allows faster access to external peripherals such as a USB drive.
  F. NTFS provides more security features.

Answer: B, F.

Explanation

The file system has no control over the speed of access or formatting of drives, and the ease of configuration is not file system-dependent.

Question 4:

A PC user issues the netstat command without any options. What is displayed as the result of this command?

    A. a historical list of successful pings that have been sent

    B. a list of all established active TCP connections

    C. a network connection and usage report

    D. a local routing table

Answer: B.

Explanation

When used by itself (without any options), the netstat command will display all the active TCP connections that are available.

Question 5:

Which two commands could be used to check if DNS name resolution is working properly on a Windows PC? (Choose two.)

    A. nslookup cisco.com

    B. net cisco.com

    C. ipconfig /flushdns

    D. nbtstat cisco.com

    E. ping cisco.com

Answer: A, E.

Explanation

The ping command tests the connection between two hosts. When ping uses a host domain name to test the connection, the resolver on the PC will first perform the name resolution to query the DNS server for the IP address of the host. If the ping command is unable to resolve the domain name to an IP address, an error will result. Nslookup is a tool for testing and troubleshooting DNS servers.

Question 6:

What is the purpose of using the net accounts command in Windows?

    A. to display information about shared network resources

    B. to show a list of computers and network devices on the network

    C. to start a network service

    D. to review the settings of password and logon requirements for users

Answer: D.

Explanation

These are some common net commands:

- **net accounts** – sets password and logon requirements for users
- **net start** – starts a network service or lists running network services
- **net use** – connects, disconnects, and displays information about shared network resources
- **net view** – shows a list of computers and network devices on the network When used without options, the net accounts command displays the current settings for password, logon limitations, and domain information

Question 7:
A technician has installed a third party utility that is used to manage a Windows 7 computer. However, the utility does not automatically start whenever the computer is started. What can the technician do to resolve this problem?
  A. Set the application registry key value to one.
  B. Use the Add or Remove Programs utility to set program access and defaults.
  C. Change the startup type for the utility to Automatic in Services.
  D. Uninstall the program and then choose Add New Programs in the Add or Remove Programs utility to install the application.

Answer: C.

Explanation
The Services console in Windows OS allows for the management of all the services on the local and remote computers. The setting of Automatic in the Services console enables the chosen service to start when the computer is started.

Question 8:
Which statement describes the function of the Server Message Block (SMB) protocol?
  A. It is used to stream media contents.
  B. It is used to manage remote PCs.
  C. It is used to compress files stored on a disk.
  D. It is used to share network resources.

Answer: D.

Explanation
The Server Message Block (SMB) protocol is primarily used by Microsoft to share network resources

Question 9:
Which statement describes a VPN?
  A. VPNs use open source virtualization software to create the tunnel through the Internet.
  B. VPNs use dedicated physical connections to transfer data between remote users.
  C. VPNs use logical connections to create public networks through the Internet.
  D. VPNs use virtual connections to create a private network through a public network.

Answer: D.

Explanation
A VPN is a private network that is created over a public network. Instead of using dedicated physical connections, a VPN uses virtual connections routed through a public network between two network devices.

Question 10:
A user logs in to Windows with a regular user account and attempts to use an application that requires administrative privileges. What can the user do to successfully use the application?
   A. Right-click the application and choose Run as Privileged.
   B. Right-click the application and choose Run as Su peruser.
   C. Right-click the application and choose Run as Administrator.
   D. Right-click the application and choose Run as root.

Answer: C.

Explanation
As a security best practice, it is advisable not to log on to Windows using the Administrator account or an account with administrative privileges. When it is necessary to run or install software that requires the privileges of the Administrator, the user can right-click the software in the Windows File Explorer and choose Run as Administrator .

Question 11:
An IT technician wants to create a rule on two Windows 10 computers to prevent an installed application from accessing the public Internet. Which tool would the technician use to accomplish this task?
   A. Local Security Policy
   B. Computer Management
   C. Windows Defender Firewall with Advanced Security
   D. DMZ

Answer: C.

Explanation
Windows Firewall with Advanced Security or the Windows 10 Windows Defender Firewall with Advanced Security is used to create inbound and outbound rules, connection security rules such as security traffic between two computers, and monitoring any active connection security rules.

Question 12:

What technology was created to replace the BIOS program on modern personal computer motherboards?
   A. UEFI
   B. MBR
   C. CMOS
   D. RAM

Answer: A.

Explanation
As of 2015, most personal computer motherboards are shipped with UEFI as the replacement for the BIOS program.

Question 13:
What is the outcome when a Linux administrator enters the man man command?
   A. The man man command configures the network interface with a manual address
   B. The man man command opens the most recent log file
   C. The man man command provides a list of commands available at the current prompt
   D. The man man command provides documentation about the man command

Answer: D.

Explanation
The man command is short for manual and is used to obtain documentation about a Linux command. The command man would provide documentation about how to use the manual.

Question 14:
What are two benefits of using an ext4 partition instead of ext3? (Choose two.)
   A. an increase in the number of supported devices
   B. improved performance
   C. compatibility with NTFS
   D. increase in the size of supported files
   E. decreased load time
   F. compatibility with CDFS

Answer: B, D.

Explanation
Based on the ex3 file system, an ext4 partition includes extensions that improve performance and an increase in the supported files. An ext4 partition also supports journaling, a file system feature that minimizes the risk of file system corruption if power is suddenly lost to the system.

Question 15:
What is the purpose of entering the netsh command on a Windows PC?

A. to configure networking parameters for the PC
B. to change the computer name for the PC
C. to create user accounts
D. to test the hardware devices on the PC

Answer: A.

Explanation
The netsh.exe tool can be used to configure networking parameters for the PC from a command prompt.

Question 16:
Which type of Windows PowerShell command performs an action and returns an output or object to the next command that will be executed?
A. cmdlets
B. functions
C. routines
D. scripts

Answer: A.

Explanation
The types of commands that PowerShell can execute include the following:
- **cmdlets** – perform an action and return an output or object to the next command that will be executed
- **PowerShell scripts** – files with a .ps1 extension that contain PowerShell commands that are executed
- **PowerShell functions** – pieces of code that can be referenced in a script

Question 17:
A user creates a file with the .ps1 extension in Windows. What type of file is it?
A. PowerShell documentation
B. PowerShell cmdlet
C. PowerShell script
D. PowerShell function

Answer: C.

Explanation
The types of commands that PowerShell can execute include the following:
- **cmdlets** – perform an action and return an output or object to the next command that will be executed
- **PowerShell scripts** – files with a .ps1 extension that contain PowerShell commands that are executed

- **PowerShell functions** – pieces of code that can be referenced in a script

Question 18:
Which Windows tool can be used by a cybersecurity administrator to secure stand-alone computers that are not part of an active directory domain?
- A. PowerShell
- B. Windows Defender
- C. Windows Firewall
- D. Local Security Policy

Answer: D.

Explanation
Windows systems that are not part of an Active Directory Domain can use the Windows Local Security Policy to enforce security settings on each stand-alone system.

Question 19:
When a wireless network in a small office is being set up, which type of IP addressing is typically used on the networked devices?
- A. private
- B. public
- C. network
- D. wireless

Answer: A.

Explanation
In setting up the wireless network in a small office, it is a best practice to use private IP addressing because of the flexibility and easy management it offers.

Question 20:
Which two parts are components of an IPv4 address? (Choose two.)
- A. logical portion
- B. host portion
- C. broadcast portion
- D. subnet portion
- E. network portion
- F. physical portion

Answer: B, E.

Explanation
An IPv4 address is divided into two parts:
- **a network portion** – to identify the specific network on which a host resides, and

- **a host portion** – to identify specific hosts on a network. A subnet mask is used to identify the length of each portion

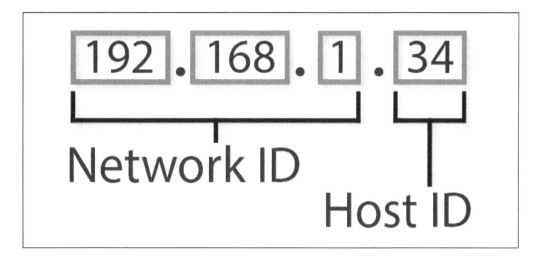

Question 21:
What is the full decompressed form of the IPv6 address 2001:420:59:0:1::a/64?
  A. 2001:4200:5900:0:1:0:0:a000
  B. 2001:0420:0059:0000:0001:0000:000a
  C. 2001:0420:0059:0000:0001:000a
  D. 2001:0420:0059:0000:0001:0000:0000:000a
  E. 2001:420:59:0:1:0:0:a
  F. 2001:4200:5900:0000:1000:0000:0000:a000

Answer: D.

Explanation
To decompress an IPv6 address, the two rules of compression must be reversed. Any 16-bit hextet that has less than four hex characters is missing the leading zeros that were removed. An IPv6 address should have a total of 8 groups of 16-bit hextets, a (::) can be replaced with consecutive zeros that were removed.

Question 22:
A cybersecurity analyst believes an attacker is spoofing the MAC address of the default gateway to perform a man-in-the-middle attack. Which command should the analyst use to view the MAC address a host is using to reach the default gateway?
  A. route print
  B. ipconfig /all
  C. netstat -r
  D. arp -a

Answer: D.

Explanation
ARP is a protocol used with IPv4 to map a MAC address to an associated specific IP address. The command arp -a will display the MAC address table on a Windows PC.

Question 23:
A user sends an HTTP request to a web server on a remote network. During encapsulation for this request, what information is added to the address field of a frame to indicate the destination?
- A. the network domain of the destination host
- B. the MAC address of the destination host
- C. the IP address of the default gateway
- D. the MAC address of the default gateway

Answer: D.

Explanation
A frame is encapsulated with source and destination MAC addresses. The source device will not know the MAC address of the remote host. An ARP request will be sent by the source and will be responded to by the router. The router will respond with the MAC address of its interface, the one which is connected to the same network as the source.

Question 24:
What addresses are mapped by ARP?
- A. destination IPv4 address lo the source MAC address
- B. destination MAC address to a destination IPv4 address
- C. destination MAC address to the source IPv4 address
- D. destination IPv4 address to the destination host name

Answer: B.

Explanation
ARP, or the Address Resolution Protocol, works by mapping a destination MAC address to a destination IPv4 address. The host knows the destination IPv4 address and uses ARP to resolve the corresponding destination MAC address.

Question 25:
What type of information is contained in an ARP table?
- A. domain name to IP address mappings
- B. switch ports associated with destination MAC addresses
- C. routes to reach destination networks
- D. IPaddressto MAC address mappings

Answer: D.

Explanation
ARP tables are used to store mappings of IP addresses to MAC addresses. When a network device needs to forward a packet, the device knows only the IP address. To deliver the packet on an Ethernet network, a MAC address is needed. ARP resolves the MAC address and stores it in an ARP table.

Question 26:
What type of information is contained in a DNS MX record?
   A. the IP address of an authoritative name server
   B. the FQDN of the alias used to identify a service
   C. the domain name mapped to mail exchange servers
   D. the IP address for an FQDN entry

Answer: C.

Explanation
MX, or mail exchange messages, are used to map a domain name to several mail exchange servers that all belong to the same domain.

Question 27:
A PC is downloading a large file from a server. The TCP window is 1000 bytes. The server is sending the file using 100-byte segments. How many segments will the server send before it requires an acknowledgment from the PC?
   A. 1000 segments
   B. 100 segments
   C. 1 segment
   D. 10 segments

Answer: D.

Explanation
With a window of 1000 bytes, the destination host accepts segments until all 1000 bytes of data have been received. Then the destination host sends an acknowledgment.

Question 28:
A user issues a ping 192.168.250.103 command and receives a response that includes a code of 1 . What does this code represent?
   A. port unreachable
   B. network unreachable
   C. protocol unreachable
   D. host unreachable

Answer: D.

Question 29:

Which two commands can be used on a Windows host to display the routing table? (Choose two.)

    A. netstat -r

    B. show ip route

    C. netstat -s

    D. route print

    E. tracert

Answer: A, D.

Explanation
- On a Windows host, the route print or netstat -r commands can be used to display the host routing table. Both commands generate the same output.
- On a router, the show ip route command is used to display the routing table.
- The netstat -s command is used to display per-protocol statistics.
- The tracert command is used to display the path that a packet travels to its destination.

Question 30:

A user issues a ping 2001:db8:FACE:39::10 command and receives a response that includes a code of 2 . What does this code represent?

    A. host unreachable

    B. port unreachable

    C. network unreachable

    D. protocol unreachable

Answer: D.

Explanation
When a host or gateway receives a packet that it cannot deliver, it can use an ICMP Destination Unreachable message to notify the source that the destination or service is unreachable. The message will include a code that indicates why the packet could not be delivered.
These are some of the Destination Unreachable codes for ICMPv4:

    0 : net unreachable

    1 : host unreachable

    2 : protocol unreachable

    3 : port unreachable

Question 31:

A worker in the records department of a hospital accidentally sends a medical record of a patient to a printer in another department. When the worker arrives at the printer, the patient record printout is missing. What breach of confidentiality does this situation describe?

    A. EMR

B. PII

C. PSI

D. PHI

Answer: D.

Explanation

Protected Health Information (PHI) includes patient name, addresses, visiting dates and more. The Health Insurance Portability and Accountability Act (HIPAA) regulates and provides severe penalties for breaches of PHI. EMRs (Electronic Medical Records) are documents created and maintained by the medical community that contain PHI. Personally identifiable information (PII) is any information that can be used to positively identify an individual, such as name and social security number. Personal Security Information (PSI) is related to information about an individual such as passwords, access keys, and account details.

Question 32:

What type of cyberwarfare weapon was Stuxnet?

    A. botnet

    B. virus

    C. worm

    D. ransomware

Answer: C.

Explanation

The Stuxnet worm was an excellent example of a sophisticated cyberwarfare weapon. In 2010, it was used to attack programmable logic controllers that operated uranium enrichment centrifuges in Iran.

Question 33:

Which example illustrates how malware might be concealed?

    A. A hacker uses techniques to improve the ranking of a website so that users are redirected to a malicious site.

    B. An attack is launched against the public website of an online retailer with the objective of blocking its response to visitors.

    C. A botnet of zombies carries personal information back to the hacker.

    D. An email is sent to the employees of an organization with an attachment that looks like an antivirus update, but the attachment actually consists of spyware.

Answer: D.

Explanation

An email attachment that appears as valid software but actually contains spyware shows how malware might be concealed. An attack to block access to a website is a DoS attack. A hacker uses search engine optimization (SEO) poisoning to improve the ranking of a website so that users are directed to a malicious site that hosts malware or uses social engineering methods to obtain information. A botnet of zombie computers is used to launch a DDoS attack.

Question 34:

In a smart home, an owner has connected many home devices to the Internet, such as the refrigerator and the coffee maker. The owner is concerned that these devices will make the wireless network vulnerable to attacks. What action could be taken to address this issue?

    A. Configure mixed mode wireless operation.

    B. Install the latest firmware versions for the devices.

    C. Assign static IP addresses to the wireless devices.

    D. Disable the SSID broadcast.

Answer: B.

Explanation
The Internet of Things (IoT) is facilitating the connection of different kinds of devices to the internet, like home devices such as coffee makers and refrigerators, and also wearable devices. In order to make these devices secure and not vulnerable to attacks, they have to be updated with the latest firmware.

Question 35:

A group of users on the same network are all complaining about their computers running slowly. After investigating, the technician determines that these computers are part of a zombie network. Which type of malware is used to control these computers?

    A. botnet

    B. spyware

    C. virus

    D. rootkit

Answer: A.

Explanation
A botnet is a network of infected computers called a zombie network. The computers are controlled by a hacker and are used to attack other computers or to steal data.

Question 36:

Which statement describes cyberwarfare?

    A. It is an Internet-based conflict that involves the penetration of information systems of other nations.

    B. It is simulation software for Air Force pilots that allows them to practice under a simulated war scenario.

    C. Cyberwarfare is an attack carried out by a group of script kiddies.

D. It is a series of personal protective equipment developed for soldiers involved in nuclear war

Answer: A.

Explanation
Cyberwarfare is Internet-based conflict that involves the penetration of the networks and computer systems of other nations. Organized hackers are typically involved in such an attack.

Question 37:
Why do IoT devices pose a greater risk than other computing devices on a network?
   A. Most IoT devices do not receive frequent firmware updates.
   B. Most IoT devices do not require an Internet connection and are unable to receive new updates.
   C. IoT devices cannot function on an isolated network with only an Internet connection.
   D. IoT devices require unencrypted wireless connections.

Answer: A.

Explanation
IoT devices commonly operate using their original firmware and do not receive updates as frequently as laptops, desktops, and mobile platforms.

Question 38:
Which cyber attack involves a coordinated attack from a botnet of zombie computers?
   A. DDoS
   B. MITM
   C. address spoofing
   D. ICMP redirect

Answer:

Explanation
DDoS is a distributed denial-of-services attack. A DDoS attack is launched from multiple coordinated sources. The sources of the attack are zombie hosts that the cybercriminal has built into a botnet. When ready, the cybercriminal instructs the botnet of zombies to attack the chosen target.

Question 39:
What is the main purpose of cyberwarfare?
   A. to protect cloud-based data centers
   B. to develop advanced network devices
   C. to gain advantage over adversaries
   D. to simulate possible war scenarios among nations

Answer: C.

Explanation
Cyberwarfare is Internet-based conflict that involves the penetration of the networks and computer systems of other nations. The main purpose of cyberwarfare is to gain advantage over adversaries, whether they are nations or competitors.

Question 40:
Why would a network administrator choose Linux as an operating system in the Security Operations Center (SOC)?
   A. It is easier to use than other operating systems.
   B. More network applications are created for this environment.
   C. It is more secure than other server operating systems.
   D. The administrator has more control over the operating system.

Answer: D.

Explanation
There are several reasons why Linux is a good choice for the SOC. Linux is open source. The command line interface is a very powerful environment. The user has more control over the operating system. Linux allows for better network communication control.

Question 41:
Which two methods can be used to harden a computing device? (Choose two.)
   A. Allow default services to remain enabled.
   B. Allow USB auto-detection.
   C. Enforce the password history mechanism.
   D. Update patches on a strict annual basis irrespective of release date.
   E. Ensure physical security.

Answer: C, E.

Explanation
The basic best practices for device hardening are as follows:
   • Step 1 - Ensure physical security.
   • Step 2 - Minimize installed packages.
   • Step 3 - Disable unused services.
   • Step 4 - Use SSH and disable the root account login over SSH.
   • Step 5 - Keep the system updated.
   • Step 6 - Disable USB auto-detection.
   • Step 7 - Enforce strong passwords.
   • Step 8 - Force periodic password changes.
   • Step 9 - Keep users from reusing old passwords.

- Step 10 - Review logs regularly.

Question 42:
Which Linux command can be used to display the name of the current working directory?
  - A. sudo
  - B. ps
  - C. pwd
  - D. chmod

Answer:

Explanation
One of the most important commands in Linux is the pwd command, which stands for print working directory. It shows users the physical path for the directory they are working in.

Question 43:
A Linux system boots into the GUI by default, so which application can a network administrator use in order to access the CLI environment?
  - A. system viewer
  - B. file viewer
  - C. package management tool
  - D. terminal emulator

Answer: D.

Explanation
A terminal emulator is an application program a user of Linux can use in order to access the CLI environment.

Question 44:
What is the well-known port address number used by DNS to serve requests?
  - A. 25
  - B. 53
  - C. 110
  - D. 60

Answer: B.

Explanation
Port numbers are used in TCP and UDP communications to differentiate between the various services running on a device. The well-known port number used by DNS is port 53.

Question 45:

Which user can override file permissions on a Linux computer?
- A. any user that has 'group' permission to the file
- B. only the creator of the file
- C. any user that has 'other' permission to the file
- D. root user

Answer: D.

Explanation
A user has as many rights to a file as the file permissions allow. The only user that can override file permission on a Linux computer is the root user. Because the root user has the power to override file permissions, the root user can write to any file.

Question 46:
What message informs IPv6 enabled interfaces to use stateful DHCPv6 for obtaining an IPv6 address?
- A. the ICMPv6 Router Solicitation
- B. the DHCPv6 Advertise message
- C. the DHCPv6 Reply message
- D. the ICMPv6 Router Advertisement

Answer: D.

Explanation
Before an IPv6 enabled interface will use stateful DHCPv6 to obtain an IPv6 address, the interface must receive an ICMPv6 Router Advertisement with the managed configuration flag (M flag) set to 1.

Question 47:
What is the purpose of ICMP messages?
- A. to inform routers about network topology changes
- B. to ensure the delivery of an IP packet
- C. to provide feedback of IP packet transmissions
- D. to monitor the process of a domain name lo IP address resolution

Answer: C.

Explanation
The purpose of ICMP messages is to provide feedback about issues that are related to the processing of IP packets.

Question 48:
What network service uses the WHOIS protocol?
- A. HTTPS

132

B. DNS
C. SMTP
D. FTP

Answer:

Explanation
WHOIS is a TCP-based protocol that is used to identify the owners of internet domains through the DNS system.

Question 49:
What action does a DHCPv4 client take if it receives more than one DHCPOFFER from multiple DHCP servers?
    A. It sends a DHCPNAK and begins the DHCP process over again.
    B. It accepts both DHCPOFFER messages and sends a DHCPACK.
    C. It discards both offers and sends a new DHCPDISCOVER.
    D. It sends a DHCPREQUEST that identifies which lease offer the client is accepting.

Answer: D.

Explanation
If there are multiple DHCP servers in a network, it is possible for a client to receive more than one DHCPOFFER. In this scenario, the client will only send one DHCPREQUEST, which includes the server from which the client is accepting the offer.

Question 50:
Refer to the exhibit. From the perspective of users behind the NAT router, what type of NAT address is 209.165.201.1?
    A. inside global
    B. inside local
    C. outside global
    D. outside local

Answer: A.

Explanation
From the perspective of users behind NAT, inside global addresses are used by external users to reach internal hosts. Inside local addresses are the addresses assigned to internal hosts. Outside global addresses are the addresses of destinations on the external network. Outside local addresses are the actual private addresses of destination hosts behind other NAT devices.

Question 51:
What is done to an IP packet before it is transmitted over the physical medium?
    A. It is tagged with information guaranteeing reliable delivery.

133

B. It is segmented into smaller individual pieces.
C. It is encapsulated in a Layer 2 frame.
D. It is encapsulated into a TCP segment.

Answer: C.

Explanation
When messages are sent on a network, the encapsulation process works from the top of the OSI or TCP/IP model to the bottom. At each layer of the model, the upper layer information is encapsulated into the data field of the next protocol. For example, before an IP packet can be sent, it is encapsulated in a data link frame at Layer 2 so that it can be sent over the physical medium.

Question 52:
Which PDU is processed when a host computer is de-encapsulating a message at the transport layer of the TCP/IP model?
   A. segment
   B. packet
   C. frame
   D. bits

Answer: A.

Explanation
At the transport layer, a host computer will de-encapsulate a segment to reassemble data to an acceptable format by the application layer protocol of the TCP/IP model.

Question 53:
Which networking model is being used when an author uploads one chapter document to a file server of a book publisher?
   A. peer-to- peer
   B. client/server
   C. master-slave
   D. point-to-point

Answer: B.

Explanation
In the client/server network model, a network device assumes the role of server in order to provide a particular service such as file transfer and storage. In the client/server network model, a dedicated server does not have to be used, but if one is present, the network model being used is the client/server model. In contrast, a peer-to-peer network does not have a dedicated server.

Question 54:
Which type of transmission is used to transmit a single video stream such as a web-based video conference to a select number of users?
   A. anycast
   B. broadcast
   C. unicast
   D. multicast

Answer: D.

Explanation
An anycast is used with IPv6 transmissions. A unicast is a transmission to a single host destination. A broadcast is a transmission sent to all hosts on a destination network.

Question 55:
What is the result of an ARP poisoning attack?
   A. Network clients are infected with a virus.
   B. Network clients experience a denial of service.
   C. Client memory buffers are overwhelmed.
   D. Client information is stolen.

Answer: D.

Explanation
ARP poisoning is a technique used by an attacker to reply to an ARP request for an IPv4 address belonging to another device, such as the default gateway. The attacker, who is effectively doing an MITM attack, pretends to be the default gateway and sends an ARP reply to the transmitter of the ARP request. The receiver of the ARP reply will add the wrong MAC address to the ARP table and will send the packets to the attacker. Therefore, all traffic to the default gateway will funnel through the attacker device.

Question 56:
What is the function of the HTTP GET message?
   A. to upload content to a web server from a web client
   B. to retrieve client email from an email server using TCP port 110
   C. to request an HTML page from a web server
   D. to send error information from a web server to a web client

Answer: C.

Explanation
There are three common HTTP message types:
   • **GET** – used by clients to request data from the web server
   • **POST** – used by clients to upload data to a web server

- **PUT** – used by clients to upload data to a web server

Question 57:
Which protocol is a client/server file sharing protocol and also a request/response protocol?
   A. FTP
   B. UDP
   C. TCP
   D. SMB

Answer: D.

Explanation
The Server Message Block (SMB) is a client/server file sharing protocol that describes the structure of shared network resources such as directories, files, printers, and serial ports. SMB is also a request/response protocol.

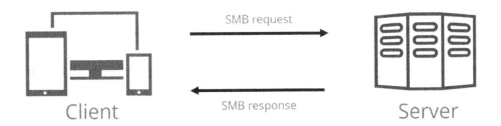

Question 58:
How is a DHCPDISCOVER transmitted on a network to reach a DHCP server?
   A. A DHCPDISCOVER message is sent with the broadcast IP address as the destination address.
   B. A DHCPDISCOVER message is sent with a multicast IP address that all DHCP servers listen to as the destination address.
   C. A DHCPDISCOVER message is sent with the IP address of the default gateway as the destination address.
   D. A DHCPDISCOVER message is sent with the IP address of the DHCP server as the destination address.

Answer: A.

Explanation
The DHCPDISCOVER message is sent by a DHCPv4 client and targets a broadcast IP along with the destination port 67. The DHCPv4 server or servers respond to the DHCPv4 clients by targeting port 68.

Question 59:
What is a description of a DNS zone transfer?
   A. transferring blocks of DNS data from a DNS server to another server
   B. the action taken when a DNS server sends a query on behalf of a DNS resolver
   C. forwarding a request from a DNS server in a subdomain to an authoritative source
   D. finding an address match and transferring the numbered address from a DNS server to the original requesting client

Answer: A.

Explanation
When a server requires data for a zone, it will request a transfer of that data from an authoritative server for that zone. The process of transferring blocks of DNS data between servers is known as a zone transfer.

Question 60:
What are the two sizes (minimum and maximum) of an Ethernet frame? (Choose two.)
   A. 128 bytes
   B. 64 bytes
   C. 1024 bytes
   D. 56 bytes
   E. 1518 bytes

Answer: B, E.

Explanation
The minimum Ethernet frame is 64 bytes. The maximum Ethernet frame is 1518 bytes. A network technician must know the minimum and maximum frame size in order to recognize runt and jumbo frames.

Question 61:
Which process failed if a computer cannot access the internet and received an IP address of 169.254.142.5?
   A. DNS
   B. IP
   C. HTTP
   D. DHCP

Answer: D.

Explanation
When a Windows computer cannot communicate with an IPv4 DHCP server, the computer automatically assigns itself an IP address in the 169.254.0.0/16 range. Linux and Apple computers do not automatically assign an IP address.

Question 62:
Which statement describes a feature of the IP protocol?
    A. IP relies on Layer 2 protocols for transmission error control.
    B. MAC addresses are used during the IP packet encapsulation.
    C. IP relies on upper layer services to handle situations of missing or out-of-order packets.
    D. IP encapsulation is modified based on network media.

Answer: C.

Explanation
IP protocol is a connectionless protocol, considered unreliable in terms of end-to-end delivery. It does not provide error control in the cases where receiving packets are out-of-order or in cases of missing packets. It relies on upper layer services, such as TCP, to resolve these issues.

Question 63:
What is a basic characteristic of the IP protocol?
    A. connectionless
    B. media dependent
    C. user data segmentation
    D. reliable end-to-end delivery

Answer: A.

Explanation
Internet Protocol (IP) is a network layer protocol that does not require initial exchange of control information to establish an end-to-end connection before packets are forwarded. Thus, IP is connectionless and does not provide reliable end-to-end delivery by itself. IP is media independent. User data segmentation is a service provided at the transport layer.

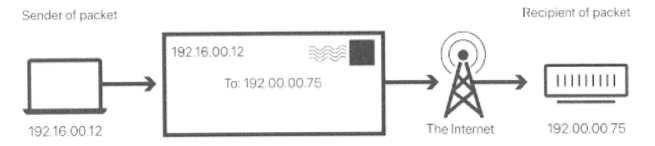

138

Question 64:
Which statement describes the ping and tracert commands?
   A. Both ping and tracert can show results in a graphical display.
   B. Ping shows whether the transmission is successful; tracert does not.
   C. Tracert shows each hop, while ping shows a destination reply only.
   D. Tracert uses IP addresses; ping does not.

Answer: C.

Explanation
The ping utility tests end-to-end connectivity between the two hosts. However, if the message does not reach the destination, there is no way to determine where the problem is located. On the other hand, the traceroute utility (tracert in Windows) traces the route a message takes from its source to the destination. Traceroute displays each hop along the way and the time it takes for the message to get to that network and back.

Question 65:
A large corporation has modified its network to allow users to access network resources from their personal laptops and smartphones. Which networking trend does this describe?
   A. cloud computing
   B. video conferencing
   C. online collaboration
   D. bring your own device

Answer: D.

Explanation
BYOD allows end users to use personal tools to access the corporate network. Allowing this trend can have major impacts on a network, such as security and compatibility with corporate software and devices.

Question 66:
Which method would an IPv6-enabled host using SLAAC employ to learn the address of the default gateway?
   A. router advertisement messages received from the link router
   B. router solicitation messages received from the link router
   C. neighbor advertisement messages received from link neighbors
   D. neighbor solicitation messages sent to link neighbors

Answer: A.

Explanation

When using SLAAC, a host will learn from the router advertisement that is sent by the link router the address to use as a default gateway.

Question 67:
A user issues a ping 192.168.250.103 command and receives a response that includes a code of 1. What does this code represent?
- A. network unreachable
- B. port unreachable
- C. protocol unreachable
- D. host unreachable

Answer: D.

Question 68:
Which AAA component can be established using token cards?
- A. authentication
- B. accounting
- C. authorization
- D. auditing

Answer: A.

Explanation
The authentication component of AAA is established using username and password combinations, challenge and response questions, and token cards. The authorization component of AAA determines which resources the user can access and which operations the user is allowed to perform. The accounting and auditing component of AAA keeps track of how network resources are used.

Question 69:
How does network scanning help assess operations security?
- A. It can detect open TCP ports on network systems.
- B. It can detect weak or blank passwords.
- C. It can simulate attacks from malicious sources.
- D. It can log abnormal activity.

Answer: A.

Explanation
Network scanning can help a network administrator strengthen the security of the network and systems by identifying open TCP and UDP ports that could be targets of an attack.

Question 70:
Which two operations are provided by TCP but not by UDP? (Choose two.)

A. retransmitting any unacknowledged data
B. acknowledging received data
C. reconstructing data in the order received
D. identifying the applications
E. tracking individual conversations

Answer: A, B.

Explanation
Numbering and tracking data segments, acknowledging received data, and retransmitting any unacknowledged data are reliability operations to ensure that all of the data arrives at the destination. UDP does not provide reliability. Both TCP and UDP identify the applications and track individual conversations. UDP does not number data segments and reconstructs data in the order that it is received.

Question 71:
What two components of traditional web security appliances are examples of functions integrated into a Cisco Web Security Appliance? (Choose two.)
A. email virus and spam filtering
B. VPN connection
C. firewall
D. web reporting
E. URL filtering

Answer: D, E.

Explanation
The Cisco Web Security Appliance is a secure web gateway which combines advanced malware protection, application visibility and control, acceptable use policy controls, reporting, and secure mobility functions. With traditional web security appliances, these functions are typically provided through multiple appliances. It is not a firewall appliance in that it only filters web traffic. It does not provide VPN connections, nor does it provide email virus and spam filtering; the Cisco Email Security Appliance provides these functions.

Question 72:
A network administrator is testing network connectivity by issuing the ping command on a router. Which symbol will be displayed to indicate that a time expired during the wait for an ICMP echo reply message?
A. U
B. .
C. !
D. $

Answer: B.

Explanation
When the ping command is issued on a router, the most common indicators are as follows:
- ! – indicates receipt of an ICMP echo reply message
- . – indicates a time expired while waiting for an ICMP echo reply message
- U – an ICMP message of unreachability was received

Question 73:
What is the function of the distribution layer of the three-layer network design model?
- A. providing direct access to the network
- B. providing secure access to the Internet
- C. aggregating access layer connections
- D. providing high speed connection to the network edge

Answer: C.

Explanation
The function of the distribution layer is to provide connectivity to services and to aggregate the access layer connections

Question 74:
At which OSI layer is a source MAC address added to a PDU during the encapsulation process?
- A. application layer
- B. presentation layer
- C. data link layer
- D. transport layer

Answer: C.

Question 75:
Which value, that is contained in an IPv4 header field, is decremented by each router that receives a packet?
- A. Time-to-Live
- B. Fragment Offset
- C. Header Length
- D. Differentiated Services

Answer: A.

Explanation
When a router receives a packet, the router will decrement the Time-to-Live (TTL) field by one. When the field reaches zero, the receiving router will discard the packet and will send an ICMP Time Exceeded message to the sender.

Question 76:
What are the three responsibilities of the transport layer? (Choose three.)

A. identifying the applications and services on the client and server that should handle transmitted data
B. conducting error detection of the contents in frames
C. meeting the reliability requirements of applications, if any
D. directing packets towards the destination network
E. formatting data into a compatible form for receipt by the destination devices
F. multiplexing multiple communication streams from many users or applications on the same network

Answer: A, C, F.

Explanation
The transport layer has several responsibilities. Some of the primary responsibilities include the following: Tracking the individual communication streams between applications on the source and destination hosts Segmenting data at the source and reassembling the data at the destination Identifying the proper application for each communication stream through the use of port numbers Multiplexing the communications of multiple users or applications over a single network Managing the reliability requirements of applications

Question 77:
Which two ICMP messages are used by both IPv4 and IPv6 protocols? (Choose two.)

A. route redirection
B. neighbor solicitation
C. router solicitation
D. router advertisement
E. protocol unreachable

Answer: A, E.

Explanation
The ICMP messages common to both ICMPv4 and ICMPv6 include: host confirmation, destination (net, host, protocol, port) or service unreachable, time exceeded, and route redirection. Router solicitation, neighbor solicitation, and router advertisement are new protocols implemented in ICMPv6.

Question 78:
What mechanism is used by a router to prevent a received IPv4 packet from traveling endlessly on a network?

A. It checks the value of the HL field and if it is 100, it discards the packet and sends a Destination Unreachable message to the source host.

B. It decrements the value of the HL field by 1 and if the result is 0, it discards the packet and sends a Time Exceeded message to the source host.
C. It checks the value of the HL field and if it is 0, it discards the packet and sends a Destination Unreachable message to the source host.
D. It increments the value of the HL field by 1 and if the result is 100, it discards the packet and sends a Parameter Problem message to the source host.

Answer: B.

Explanation
To prevent an IPv4 packet from traveling in the network endlessly, TCP/IP protocols use ICMPv4 protocol to provide feedback about issues. When a router receives a packet and decrements the TTL field in the IPv4 packet by 1 and if the result is zero, it discards the packet and sends a Time Exceeded message to the source host.

Question 79:
A device has been assigned the IPv6 address of 2001:0db8:cafe:4500:1000:00d8:0058:00ab/64. Which is the host identifier of the device?
   A. 2001:0db8:cafe:4500:1000:00d8:0058:00ab
   B. 00ab
   C. 2001:0db8:cafe:4500
   D. 1000:00d8:0058:00ab

Answer: D.

Explanation
The address has a prefix length of /64. Thus the first 64 bits represent the network portion, whereas the last 64 bits represent the host portion of the IPv6 address.

Question 80:
What three application layer protocols are part of the TCP/IP protocol suite? (Choose three.)
   A. DHCP
   B. PPP
   C. FTP
   D. DNS
   E. NAT
   F. ARP

Answer: A, C, D,

Explanation

DNS, DHCP, and FTP are all application layer protocols in the TCP/IP protocol suite. ARP and PPP are network access layer protocols, and NAT is an internet layer protocol in the TCP/IP protocol suite.

Question 81:

A computer can access devices on the same network but cannot access devices on other networks. What is the probable cause of this problem?
   A. The computer has an invalid IP address.
   B. The cable is not connected properly to the NIC.
   C. The computer has an incorrect subnet mask.
   D. The computer has an invalid default gateway address.

Answer: D.

Explanation
The default gateway is the address of the device a host uses to access the Internet or another network. If the default gateway is missing or incorrect, that host will not be able to communicate outside the local network. Because the host can access other hosts on the local network, the network cable and the other parts of the IP configuration are working.

Question 82:

A user who is unable to connect to the file server contacts the help desk. The helpdesk technician asks the user to ping the IP address of the default gateway that is configured on the workstation. What is the purpose for this ping command?
   A. to resolve the domain name of the file server to its IP address
   B. to request that gateway forward the connection request to the file server
   C. to obtain a dynamic IP address from the server
   D. to test that the host has the capability to reach hosts on other networks

Answer: D.

Explanation
The ping command is used to test connectivity between hosts. The other options describe tasks not performed by ping . Pinging the default gateway will test whether the host has the capability to reach hosts on its own network and on other networks

Question 83:

A user gets an IP address of 192.168.0.1 from the company network administrator. A friend of the user at a different company gets the same IP address on another PC. How can two PCs use the same IP address and still reach the Internet, send and receive email, and search the web?
   A. ISPs use Domain Name Service to change a user IP address into a public IP address that can be used on the Internet.
   B. Both users must be using the same Internet Service Provider.

C. Both users must be on the same network.

D. ISPs use Network Address Translation to change a user IP address into an address that can be used on the Internet.

Answer: D.

Explanation

As user traffic from behind an ISP firewall reaches the gateway device, Network Address Translation changes private IP addresses into a public, routable IP address. Private user addresses remain hidden from the public Internet, and thus more than one user can have the same private IP address, regardless of ISP.

Question 84:
How many host addresses are available on the 192.168.10.128/26 network?
   A. 30
   B. 32
   C. 60
   D. 62
   E. 64

Answer: D.

Explanation

A /26 prefix gives 6 host bits, which provides a total of 64 addresses, because 2 6 = 64. Subtracting the network and broadcast addresses leaves 62 usable host addresses.

Question 85:
What are the three ranges of IP addresses that are reserved for internal private use? (Choose three.)
   A. 64.100.0.0/14
   B. 192.168.0.0/16
   C. 192.31.7.0/24
   D. 172.16.0.0/12
   E. 10.0.0.0/8
   F. 127.16.0.0/12

Answer: B, D, E.

Explanation

The private IP address blocks that are used inside companies are as follows:10.0.0.0 /8 (any address that starts with 10 in the first octet) 172.16.0.0 /12 (any address that starts with 172.16 in the first two octets through 172.31.255.255) 192.168.0.0 /16 (any address that starts with 192.168 in the first two octets)

Question 86:
A host PC is attempting to lease an address through DHCP. What message is sent by the server to let the client know it is able to use the provided IP information?
  A. DHCPDISCOVER
  B. DHCPOFFER
  C. DHCPREQUEST
  D. DHCPACK
  E. DHCPNACK

Answer: D.

Explanation
When a host uses DHCP to automatically configure an IP address, it typically sends two messages: the DHCPDISCOVER message and the DHCPREQUEST message. These two messages are usually sent as broadcasts to ensure that all DHCP servers receive them. The servers respond to these messages using DHCPOFFER, DHCPACK, and DHCPNACK messages, depending on the circumstance

Question 87:
An employee complains that a Windows PC cannot connect to the Internet. A network technician issues the ipconfig command on the PC and is shown an IP address of 169.254.10.3. Which two conclusions can be drawn? (Choose two.)
  A. The PC is configured to obtain an IP address automatically.
  B. The default gateway address is not configured.
  C. The DNS server address is misconfigured.
  D. The enterprise network is misconfigured for dynamic routing.
  E. The PC cannot contact a DHCP server.

Answer: A, E.

Explanation
When a Windows PC is configured to obtain an IP address automatically, the PC will try to obtain an IP address from a DHCP server. When the PC cannot contact a DHCP server, Windows will automatically assign an address belonging to the 169.254.0.0/16 range.

Question 88:
What is a function of the tracert command that differs from the ping command when they are used on a workstation?
  A. The tracert command is used to test the connectivity between two devices.
  B. The tracert command reaches the destination faster.
  C. The tracert command shows the information of routers in the path.
  D. The tracert command sends one ICMP message to each hop in the path.

Answer: C.

Explanation
The tracert command sends three pings to each hop (router) in the path toward the destination and displays the domain name and IP address of hops from their responses. Because tracert uses the ping command, the travel time is the same as a standalone ping command. The primary function of a standalone ping command is to test the connectivity between two hosts.

Question 89:
Which two functions or operations are performed by the MAC sublayer? (Choose two.)
    A. It is responsible for Media Access Control.
    B. It performs the function of NIC driver software.
    C. It adds a header and trailer to form an OSI Layer 2 PDU.
    D. It handles communication between upper and lower layers.
    E. It adds control information to network protocol layer data.

Answer: A, C.

Explanation
The MAC sublayer is the lower of the two data link sublayers and is closest to the physical layer. The two primary functions of the MAC sublayer are to encapsulate the data from the upper layer protocols and to control access to the media.

Question 90:
Which field in an IPv4 packet header will typically stay the same during its transmission?
    A. Flag
    B. Time-to-Live
    C. Packet Length
    D. Destination Address

Answer: D.

Explanation
The value in the Destination Address field in an IPv4 header will stay the same during its transmission. The other options might change during its transmission.

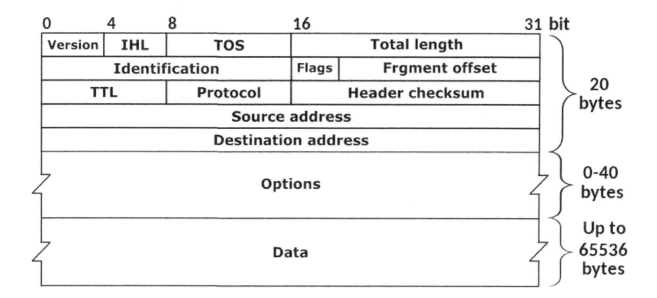

Question 91:
What is an advantage of HIPS that is not provided by IDS?
    A. HIPS protects critical system resources and monitors operating system processes.
    B. HIPS deploys sensors at network entry points and protects critical network segments.
    C. HIPS monitors network processes and protects critical files.
    D. HIPS provides quick analysis of events through detailed logging.

Answer: A.

Explanation
Network-based IDS (NIDS) sensors are typically deployed in offline mode. They do not protect individual hosts. Host-based IPS (HIPS) is software installed on a single host to monitor and analyze suspicious activity. It can monitor and protect operating systems and critical system processes that are specific to that host. HIPS can be thought of as a combination of antivirus software, antimalware software, and a firewall.

Question 92:
Which statement describes a difference between RADIUS and TACACS+?
    A. RADIUS separates authentication and authorization whereas TACACS+ combines them as one process.
    B. RADIUS is supported by the Cisco Secure ACS software whereas TACACS+ is not.
    C. RADIUS uses TCP whereas TACACS+ uses UDP.
    D. RADIUS encrypts only the password whereas TACACS+ encrypts all communication.

Answer: D.

Explanation

TACACS+ uses TCP, encrypts the entire packet (not just the password), and separates authentication and authorization into two distinct processes. Both protocols are supported by the Cisco Secure ACS software.

Question 93:
What are two disadvantages of using an IDS? (Choose two.)
   A. The IDS does not stop malicious traffic.
   B. The IDS works offline using copies of network traffic.
   C. The IDS has no impact on traffic.
   D. The IDS analyzes actual forwarded packets.
   E. The IDS requires other devices to respond to attacks.

Answer: A, E.

Explanation
The disadvantage of operating with mirrored traffic is that the IDS cannot stop malicious single-packet attacks from reaching the target before responding to the attack. Also, an IDS often requires assistance from other networking devices, such as routers and firewalls, to respond to an attack. An advantage of an IDS is that by working offline using mirrored traffic, it has no impact on traffic flow.

Question 94:
Which statement describes one of the rules that govern interface behavior in the context of implementing a zone-based policy firewall configuration?
   A. An administrator can assign interfaces to zones, regardless of whether the zone has been configured.
   B. An administrator can assign an interface to multiple security zones.
   C. By default, traffic is allowed to flow among interfaces that are members of the same zone.
   D. By default, traffic is allowed to flow between a zone member interface and any interface that is not a zone member.

Answer: C.

Explanation
An interface can belong to only one zone. Creating a zone is the first step in configuring a zone-based policy firewall. A zone cannot be assigned to an interface if the zone has not been created. Traffic can never flow between an interface that is assigned to a zone and an interface that has not been assigned to a zone

Question 95:
What is a host-based intrusion detection system (HIDS)?
   A. It detects and stops potential direct attacks but does not scan for malware.
   B. It is an agentless system that scans files on a host for potential malware.

C. It identifies potential attacks and sends alerts but does not stop the traffic.

D. It combines the functionalities of antimalware applications with firewall protection.

Answer: D.

Explanation

A Current HIDS is a comprehensive security application that combines the functionalities of antimalware applications with firewall protection. An HIDS not only detects malware but also prevents it from executing. Because the HIDS runs directly on the host, it is considered an agent-based system.

Host Intrusion Detection System (HIDS)

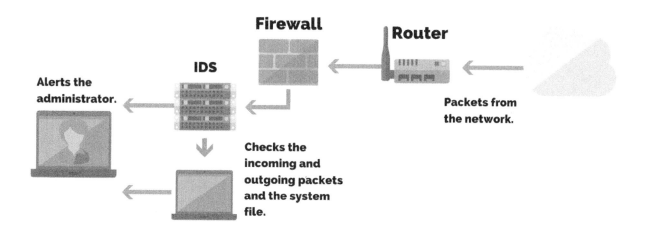

Notes

Notes

Made in United States
Orlando, FL
07 March 2023

30798808R00085